Gestures

World
Book Night
23 April

**This book was given on
World Book Night 2023
By
Cornwall College Learning Centres**

World Book Night is the national
celebration of reading that takes
place annually across the UK. Run by
The Reading Agency, it brings people
together to celebrate the difference
that reading makes to people's lives,
and to tackle life's big challenges
through the proven power of reading.

#worldbooknight
worldbooknight.org

THE
READING
AGENCY

— Because everything changes when we read

Other Books by Roger E. Axtell

Do's and Taboos Around the World: A Guide to International Behavior,
   3rd Edition

Do's and Taboos of International Trade: A Small Business Primer,
   Revised Edition

Do's and Taboos of Hosting International Visitors

Do's and Taboos of Public Speaking

Do's and Taboos of Preparing for Your Trip Abroad (with John P. Healy)

Do's and Taboos of Using English Around the World

Do's and Taboos Around the World for Women in Business
   (with Tami Briggs, Margaret Corcoran, and Mary Beth Lamb)

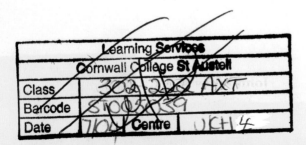

Gestures

The Do's and Taboos of Body Language Around the World

REVISED AND EXPANDED EDITION

Roger E. Axtell

Illustrations by Mike Fornwald

John Wiley & Sons, Inc.

New York • Chichester • Weinheim • Brisbane • Singapore • Toronto

This text is printed on acid-free paper.

Library of Congress Cataloging-in-Publication Data

Axtell, Roger E.
    Gestures : the do's and taboos of body language around the world / Roger E. Axtell. — Rev. and expanded ed.
      p. cm.
    Includes bibliographical references and index.
    ISBN 0-471-18342-3 (pbk. : alk. paper)
    1. Body language—Cross-cultural studies. 2. Gesture—Cross-cultural studies. 3. Nonverbal communication—Cross-cultural studies. I. TItle.
BF637.N66A88 1997
153.6'9—dc21   97-29043

Printed in the United States of America

10 9 8 7 6

To Mardi, Kathi, and Roger . . .

No mere gesture here.
I want to record it clearly for you to know:
I am proud of each of you . . .
and love you even more.

Contents

Preface

Since 1991, when the first edition of this book was published, it has become obvious that people around the world find the subject of gestures and body language of more than ordinary interest. Consider these events:

- When President George Bush visited Australia on a state visit in 1993, as he passed crowds of Aussies he flashed the "V" for Victory sign from the backseat of his limousine. Unfortunately, he did it *backward* that is, with the back of his hand facing the people. The next day his picture appeared in newspapers from Sydney to Perth with the headline "President Insults Australians." Bush was obviously unaware that in Australia, as in England, that particular signal—the reverse "V"—signifies "Up yours, mate!" The correct form is to have the palm face outward. (See page 47.) News media in the United States reported on Bush's gaffe, referring to this book for clarification.

- The first edition of *Gestures* also generated four separate appearances for the author on ABC's *Good Morning America* TV show. On the first visit, the author stood alongside the show's host, Charles Gibson, and explained that in the Middle East and Southeast Asia it was a common sign of respect and friendship for two men to walk down the street hand-in-hand . . . and then he took Gibson's hand to demonstrate. In obvious discomfort, Gibson laughed nervously, leaned toward the camera, and explained, "Roger and I have just met." The studio crew burst into laughter.

- One of the most popular daytime talk shows on Canadian national television is the *Dini Petty Show*. As Ms. Petty was interviewing the author and demonstrating some gestures, she said, "The one I liked most was this one" (and she tapped her two forefingers stiffly on a tabletop). When the author confessed he didn't recognize that gesture, Petty said, "Oh, it's in your book! You said that in Egypt it means 'I want to go to bed with you.' " The author corrected her, saying, "No, no. You go like this," and he held his forefingers outward and tapped them against each other (see page 110). Petty quickly rejoined, "Well, no wonder I didn't have any fun there!!"

- Former late-night TV host Arsenio Hall also discovered the book in 1993. One evening, in his opening monologue, Hall chastised the author about the three most popular gestures in America: the "O.K." sign, the "V" for Victory sign, and the thumbs-up. Hall said, "I think Roger is missing a very important one—you know, the one we see out here in Los Angeles on the expressways. It's kind of signaling 'We're Number One' . . . but with a different finger." And, on a separate occasion, when Johnny Carson hosted his own nightly show, he read excerpts, commenting, "It says here that in Japan, don't stand with your hands in your pockets . . . or, for that matter, in anyone else's pockets!"

- Finally, are we North Americans the only ones interested in gestures and body language? Apparently not. In the past five years this book has also appeared on bookshelves in England and Australia and has been, or is being, translated into eleven foreign languages: Finnish, French, German, Hungarian, Japanese, Korean, Portuguese, Spanish, Swedish, and two separate forms for Taiwan and mainland China. *(Author's note: I must admit to being curious how the phrase "Up yours!" was translated in each of those languages.)*

In this new, revised, and expanded second edition you will find . . . well, you'll find just that: new, revised, and updated information, and more of what was contained in the first edition. In Chapter 1, titled "The Power of Gestures," a dozen new examples of the power of gestures are provided. In Chapter 2, "The Most Popular Gestures," new information has been inserted on each of our most commonly used signals. And in Chapter 4, "Gestures: Head to Toe," and Chapter 7, "Country-by-Country Listing," you will find additional information to help you more effectively signal yourself around the world.

An entirely new section, "Special Types of Gestures" (Chapter 3), has also been added. It describes four categories of special gestures— American Sign Language, *tai chi*, flirting, and kissing—and offers a challenge to readers, which will tap your creativity skills in developing new and needed gestures.

In producing this second edition, special thanks should go to author and research specialist *Margaret Corcoran* of St. Paul, Minnesota. From 1993 to 1996, the author collaborated with Margaret and two other women in writing the book *Do's and Taboos around the World for Women in Business* (Wiley, 1997). Margaret proved to be such a competent and talented writer that it was obvious her skills would also enhance this new edition. For this new edition of *Gestures*, Margaret undertook to method-ically check and expand Chapter 7, "Country-by-Country Listing." Margaret sent questionnaires to 150 embassies, consulates, honorary consuls, friends, and cross-cultural specialists around the United States asking for suggestions for changes to the first edition. "It was gratifying to learn that most of the information in the first edition is very accurate," she reported. "And it was interesting, if not a bit frustrating, to also discover the degree to which gestures and body language can vary *within a* country among different regions, ethnic groups, social ranks, and even families."

As for illustrations, the talented Milwaukee artist *Mike Fornwald* has once again provided additional drawings of new gestures. Mike has created twenty-one new, clever, and eye-catching illustrations for this second edition.

Thanks also go to the folks at John Wiley & Sons, Publishers (New York), for commissioning this second edition, and specifically to Assistant Editor *Chris Jackson* for his encouragement, guidance, and supervision.

For future editions, if you would like to contribute your own anecdotes and experiences with gestures and body language around the world, send your offerings to:

Roger Axtell
c/o John Wiley & Sons, Publishers
605 Third Avenue
New York, NY 10158-0012

Acknowledgments

Any book on gestures and cross-cultural communication owes an impossible indebtedness to one man, Desmond Morris, and to one unrelated institution, the David M. Kennedy Center for International Studies at Brigham Young University, Provo, Utah.

Desmond Morris is a British social anthropologist, a keen observer of the human condition, and a prolific writer on the subject of both human and animal behavior. In 1977, Morris produced a glorious book titled *Manwatching* (H. N. Abrams). He followed that in 1979 with *Gestures* (Stein and Day), which carefully catalogs twenty common gestures found in Europe. In 1994, he authored *Bodytalk* (Crown). Anyone interested in a more scholarly treatment on all aspects of gestures and body language would be enriched by studying each of these.

At the David M. Kennedy Center for International Studies at Brigham Young University, *V. Lynn Tyler* has unselfishly helped me with each of my books. He is a kind, generous, and gracious man, and the Kennedy Center contains a rich supply of material on cross-cultural behavior and communication. The center offers a treasure of information to the public. One of the gems in its collection is called *Culturgrams,* a series of four-page newsletters, one for each of about 100 different countries. *Culturgrams* provides easily digestible information for each country on customs and courtesies, the people, the lifestyle, the nation, and references for additional study. Write to the Publication Services, David M. Kennedy Center for International Studies, 280 HRCB, Brigham Young University, Provo, Utah 84602 for information on *Culturgrams* and a complete listing of their many other publications.

Mike Fornwald's great talent is evident in the drawings throughout this book. His years of training and discipline in illustrating for animated films, plus his skill in political cartooning, enhanced his illustrations for this book. Moreover, he has been a delightful collaborator at every step while also freelancing for several prominent midwestern advertising agencies and publishing his own book.

A corps of others assisted me with information and by helping to check and recheck the hundreds of gestural entries throughout this book.

Susan Van Mell, a professional market researcher, contacted numerous embassies in the United States for affirmation, corrections, and additions to our research.

I met *Ingeborg Hegenbart* in Charlotte, North Carolina, in 1987, and both my writing and speaking careers have benefited ever since. Ingeborg is vice president of South Trust Bank Int'l., and as energetic and knowledgeable as one person can be in international business. She is also Dutch by birth, accent, and inclination, and helped me check and verify every entry pertaining to the Netherlands.

For things Italian, I turned to the fabulous *Fantacci* family, friends and business associates for thirty-five years. The patriarch, Giuseppe, must have provided the model for the wonderfully warm "Most Unforgettable Characters" series in the *Reader's Digest* magazine of many years ago. "Beppe" has been an inspiration to me, and his son, Bert, a great and much admired friend.

For material on Latin America, I received great assistance from *Jack* and *Marie Ottiker*, lifelong residents of that area. Marie is an accomplished writer and Jack is a former executive with several major U.S. corporations. He is more recently president of the American Chamber of Commerce in Lima, Peru.

Professor Robert T. Moran is, in my view, the preeminent educator in cross-cultural behavior, especially for business. Bob is professor of International Studies and director of the Program in Cross-Cultural Communication at "Thunderbird," officially known as the American Graduate School of International Management, Glendale, Arizona. He and Philip R. Harris coauthored the textbook *Managing Cultural Differences* (Gulf Publishing Co., 3rd ed., 1991).

Barbara Moebius is program director of the International Trade Program at the Waukesha County Technical College, Pewaukee, Wisconsin. Barb has not only developed probably the best repository of international business research material in the Midwest but has also directed a burgeoning program of training young people for lifetime careers in international business.

Eugene Theroux is an internationally known legal expert, especially on the People's Republic of China and Russia. Gene is also an equally talented writer and artist. He, along with Fredric M. Kaplan, wrote *The HarperCollins Business Guide to Moscow* (Harper & Row, 1990), an indispensable guide to anyone traveling to that city.

To review my research on gestures in Scandinavia, I turned to a thirty-year friend and business associate named *Klavs Olsen* of Copenhagen. Klavs not only has extensive business interests in Norway, Sweden, and Finland but served as president of the Danish Association of Business (comparable to a Chamber of Commerce in the United States).

To all of the above, I offer a deep Japanese bow, an Irish tip of the hat, a hearty Chinese toast, and a good old-fashioned American salute . . . gestures all, in gratitude and thanks.

Last, my most valuable resource, asset, partner, and best earthly friend (also, my collaborator in producing three wonderful children) has been, and is, my wife, Mitzi. I owe her more—much more—than mere acknowledgments.

ROGER E. AXTELL

Janesville, Wisconsin

Introduction

Over the past decade, I have presented hundreds of speeches, seminars, and workshops on the often amusing subject of international behavior. I found myself automatically saving the segment on gestures for the end of each presentation because audiences seemed to enjoy it so much. After these programs, people invariably came to me to relate their own amusing, provocative, and sometimes distressing experiences with gestures and body language around the globe.

No market research could so clearly substantiate interest in this subject. This book, then, results from an accumulation of more than ten years of research, including recent research visits to England, Germany, France, the former Yugoslavia, Greece, Italy, Hong Kong, Thailand, Malaysia, Indonesia, and the Philippines.

All this reinforced a conviction that gestures are powerful communicators used by a wide and growing number of internationally cosmopolitan individuals. One has only to view a current news show on television to see the importance of gestures in our culture as Saudis, Russians, Chinese, and numerous others speak into the ubiquitous camera.

How This Book Is Organized

This book is divided into seven chapters. The premise of Chapter 1, illustrated with numerous examples, is that not only are gestures and body language powerful communicators, but different cultures use gestures and body language in dramatically different ways.

Chapter 2 discusses the most popular gestures found around the world, beginning with how we *greet* one another. Shaking hands is by no means a universal greeting; in fact, there are at least a half-dozen other social greetings—even several different ways of shaking hands.

We next deal with "beckoning" gestures. Different cultures have different ways to relay the message "Hey! Come here." For example, on one occasion in Buenos Aires, when my host dropped me off at the hotel entrance, I waved good-bye as he drove away. To my amazement he stopped the car, got out, and came back and asked what I wanted. With that incident, I learned that waving good-bye American-style could in

Argentina actually mean "Hey! Come back." (See pages 25–26 for a more complete explanation.)

The next discussion focuses on "insulting" gestures from around the world. We include this discussion not to increase your repertoire but to help you avoid embarrassment. Gestures you probably employ safely and routinely each day are considered not only rude but obscene in certain other parts of the world.

Following that, you will find a useful exposition on *touching*. While some cultures eschew bodily contact in almost all business and social situations, others actually expect it.

Chapter 2 also takes four common gestures and illustrates the *yin* and *yang* (or opposite) meanings of each, depending on where you are in the world. Those four common gestures are: (1) The "O.K." signal—thumb and forefinger forming a circle, with the other three fingers splayed outward; (2) the "thumbs-up" gesture; (3) the "V" for Victory signal—index and middle finger forming a V; and (4) the "vertical horns," or what we have chosen to call the "hook 'em horns" gesture—a fist with the index and little fingers extended. Each of these four gestures is illustrated and examined anecdotally. My hope is that through stories and drawings, you can see how seemingly common gestures like these can get you into a world of trouble.

In Chapter 3 you will find two facets of gestures and body language that you probably know little about: American Sign Language (ASL) and *tai chi*, the Asian form of exercise. And then you will read about two more types of gestures and body language that you have probably thought about often—flirting and kissing. In all four cases, it is likely that you will learn something new. Finally, at the conclusion of Chapter 3, there is a "Challenge to Readers" (you). It invites you to help create two new gestures that should be added to our panorama of signals. This entire chapter is new and written especially for this revised, expanded edition of the book.

Chapter 4 is designed to help you learn or trace a particular gesture, using scores of drawings from the talented hand and art board of illustrator Mike Fornwald. To help you track down a specific gesture or action, Chapter 4 is organized from head to toe, literally. Therefore, if you want to know about a particular gesture you observed involving, say, the chin, you can readily find it between mouth and arms.

Chapter 5 describes what I have chosen to call the "Ultimate Gesture."

Chapter 6 provides a short list of important gestures to bear in mind.

In Chapter 7, you will find a country-by-country listing of common gestures and body language. The countries are grouped by major geographic region, starting with Europe, then the Middle East and Africa, followed by the Pacific and Asia, Central and South America, and finally the

United States and Canada. This listing not only catalogs the commonly used gestures in each but cross-references them back to Chapter 4. Therefore, if you read a word description of a gesture in the country-by-country section and are unclear about what it looks like, you can examine an illustration of it in Chapter 4.

Now, an important disclaimer.

Any book on understanding human behavior is tricky stuff. No two people behave in precisely the same way. Nor do people from the same culture all perform exactly the same gestures and body language uniformly. For almost any gesture in this book there will probably be a minority within a given nationality who might say, "Well, some might attach that meaning to it, but to me it means . . ." and then they will provide a different interpretation.

So, even among a single nationality, when dealing with hand and body signals, you will probably encounter that type of contradiction and clutter.

The clutter aside, the chief objective of this book is to help you learn *right* from *rude,* to help avoid misunderstandings.

The hope is that this book will enable you to become more sensitive, more aware, and more observant when it comes to effective, silent communications.

What is the value of avoiding just one misunderstanding? As a wise counselor once told me: "That's like trying to determine the value of a single light bulb. Unlit, the bulb has little value. Lit, the bulb can illuminate one room. And, one illuminated room occupied by one creative person can change the world."

1

The Power of Gestures

News item:

This news report appeared in the Sunday *New York Times* on August 18, 1996, and prompted *Times* writer John Kifner to ask the question, "What had the shipping minister done to provoke such wrath?" Kifner explained: "He gave the old thumbs-up." Kifner then followed with a lengthy exposition, complete with drawings, on the meanings of other innocent American gestures that can be misinterpreted overseas. His source, by the way, was the first edition of this book.

More and more Americans, along with our neighbors in the global village, are discovering the power—and the surprises—of gestures and body language.

Just look around you.

The world is a giddy montage of vivid gestures—traffic police, street vendors, expressway drivers, teachers, children on playgrounds, athletes with their exuberant hugging, clenched fists, and high fives. People all over the world use their hands, heads, and bodies to communicate expressively.

Without gestures, our world would be static, colorless. The social anthropologist Edward T. Hall claims 60 percent of *all* our communication is nonverbal. And in Daniel Goleman's international bestseller, *Emotional Intelligence* (Bantam, 1995), he claims that 90 percent of our emotions are expressed nonverbally. In that case, how can we possibly communicate with one another without gestures?

We use gestures daily, almost instinctively, from beckoning to a waiter or punctuating a business presentation with visual signals to airport ground attendants guiding an airline pilot into the jetway or a parent using a whole dictionary of gestures to teach (or preach to) a child.

Gestures can be menacing (two drivers on a freeway), warm (an open-armed welcome), instructive (a policeman giving road directions), or even sensuous (the languid movements of a Hawaiian hula dancer).

The premise of this book is not only that gestures are woven inextricably into our social lives but also that the "vocabulary" of gestures can be at once informative and entertaining . . . but also dangerous. For while great enjoyment can come from learning the odd, sometimes contradictory meanings of gestures we tend to take for granted, some innocent-appearing gestures can generate genuine grief.

Examples

An American teenager was hitchhiking in Nigeria. A carload of locals passed him. The car screeched to a halt. The locals jumped out and promptly roughed up the visitor. Why? Because in Nigeria, the gesture commonly used in America for hitchhiking (thumb extended upward) is considered a very rude signal.

Halfway around the world, an American couple on an auto tour in Australia was stopped by a policeman in Sydney for failing to signal before turning. Seeing that they were tourists, the officer gave them only a friendly warning. Relieved, the American man responded with a smile and the thumbs-up sign. The policeman became enraged, ordered the couple out of the car, called a backup, searched the car, and finally gave the driver an expensive ticket. Later, back in their hotel and recounting their experience, the tourists learned that in Australia the thumbs-up gesture means "screw you!"

And so we see that the same American gesture (signifying "Great!") has dire consequences in Australia as in Nigeria, a half world away.

Conversely, gestures can simply be fun, impulsive, and irresistible.

Examples

In 1990, *National Geographic Magazine* lined up all the members of the U.S. Supreme Court for an official photograph. Justice Sandra Day O'Connor found herself standing behind Justice Byron White. According to news reports, Justice O'Connor apparently could not resist the impulse shared by children and adults for decades—she quietly formed a "V" with her fingers and held them just above White's head, forming the old "rabbit ears" sign. Even the loftiest jurists in the land cannot resist the urge to flash an impish gesture from time to time.

And, speaking of lofty people, former First Lady Barbara Bush also experienced an incident where a particular gesture played tricks. In an interview on life at the White House she described being seated at a state dinner next to Russian president Boris Yeltsin who, she learned later, turned to his interpreter and asked, "What does it mean in the United

States when a woman places her foot on a man's foot," adding that "in my country it means the woman loves the man." The reason for Yeltsin's query was that, without realizing it, Mrs. Bush had been grinding his foot into the ground with her own foot. Later, Yeltsin autographed his menu with this note to Mrs. Bush: "You stepped on my foot, you knew what it meant, and I felt the same way."

Gestures and body language communicate as effectively as words—maybe even more effectively. Take a baby's smile. Can words possibly duplicate that wonderfully unique sight? It is not by accident, it seems, that as infants we learn the signal of smiling before we learn to talk. Also, according to a 1991 report in *Science* magazine, deaf babies "babble" with their hands in the same way hearing babies string sounds together before they learn to speak. Deaf babies form repetitive signals with their hands before they are ten months old, paralleling hearing infants who begin trying out sounds that evolve into spoken language.

Some anthropologists divide our actions and gestures into three broad categories: instinctive, coded, and acquired.

- *Instinctive* gestures are those we do almost unconsciously. For example, Desmond Morris writes that when humans around the world greet one another we all do the "eyebrow flash"—that is, we automatically raise our eyebrows and wrinkle our foreheads. This, he says, is a signal of openness where we are leaving the eyes unprotected. Another common instinctive gesture is when we are suddenly shocked or surprised: We tend to slap the back of our heads. A subcategory is found among psychologists who claim that certain unconscious body movements are telltale signs of what is going on inside a person's mind. For example, when one crosses one's arms in front of the chest, it is a signal of defensiveness. On the other hand, perhaps the person is merely chilly. Some followers of this school also suggest that scratching one's nose can sometimes be an indicator that a person is telling a lie. Or maybe that person's nose itches. If this branch of subconscious gestures and body language interests you, I suggest you read Julius Fast's book, *Body Language* (MJF Books), first published in 1970. Over 3 million copies of this book have been sold in ensuing years.

- *Coded*, or technical, gestures are created by preestablished agreement. Examples are hand signals used by TV directors, referees, umpires, and brokers in the stock and commodity markets. Also, as every schoolchild knows, Native Americans developed a signing system that was widely used among separate tribes and then later with the first white settlers. Today, perhaps the best-known coded language is

American Sign Language, which, as you'll learn in Chapter 3, is the third most popular language in the United States after English and Spanish.

- *Acquired* gestures, meaning our socially generated and acquired gestures, will be the focus of this book. Many of these gestures have no known origins (e.g., the "O.K." sign) or no rhyme or reason (e.g., waving the hand, as in hello or good-bye). Others can have only loose connections with their meaning (e.g., the phallic symbol can be signaled in several different ways). This grouping of gestures has been loosely and informally collected among separate societies with no particular logic except that they are widely used and understood among a certain group of people.

And that is the crux of this book. Identical gestures often mean different things among different societies. Each culture seems to adopt its own set of rules. As we just learned, in America holding a thumb upright means "Great!" and is also a hitchhiker's sign, but in Nigeria it is an insult. Which is correct? The answer depends on *where* you are.

Example

Nowhere in the United States, or in many other countries for that matter, can a person in any public situation casually pat or pinch another person on his or her derriere. In Rome, on the famous Via Veneto, a pinch may be accepted with impunity, but it's absolutely forbidden in other places around the world. In fact, in many places one might even get arrested for trying it.

But there is one exception—an aberration that occurs among football players in America (and soccer players in Europe). Surely you've noticed; from defensive back to tight end, these bruisers seem to have a fetish for fanny-patting. To compliment a teammate or exhort him to play harder, hulking linemen on American professional football teams slap the rumps of other team members. And it is perfectly acceptable behavior. But—and this is important—while they can pat and slap, *they must never linger!* That would send quite a different signal indeed.

THE SCIENCE OF GESTURES

Next time you step on to an elevator, try this experiment. It demonstrates how, even in the most mundane situations, we have a silent set of rules for bodily behavior in public settings.

Here is the setting:

If there are only one or two people on an elevator, they usually
lean against the walls of the elevator. If four people board the elevator, the four corners are usually occupied.

However, when the population reaches five or six people,
everyone begins to obey more complex rules of elevator etiquette. It is almost like a ritualistic dance. They all turn to face
the door. "They get taller and thinner," as psychologist Layne
Longfellow describes it. "Hands and purses and briefcases hang
down in front of the body—that's called The Fig Leaf Position,
by the way. They mustn't touch each other in any way unless the
elevator is crowded, and then only at the shoulder or lightly
against the upper arm. Also, there is a tendency to look upward
at the illuminated floor indicator. If they speak, it is definitely
sotto voce."

If you doubt this is standard—almost sacred—elevator
behavior, then try this. Next time you walk on to a crowded elevator, *don't turn around and face the door*. Instead, just stand there
facing the others. If you want to create even more tension, grin.
Very likely the other passengers will glare back, surprised, grim,
and upset. Reason? You have broken the rules.

One person who tried this experiment actually heard someone in the back
of the elevator whisper. "Call 911. We've got a real weirdo here."

When I related all this to my son, at the time a psychology major at
the University of Texas, he expressed disbelief. "Is that really true? I'll ask
my professor about it." A week later, he called back excitedly: "Dad, it
works. I told my professor and we decided to make it a class experiment
by trying it in office buildings here. We've got people freaking out on elevators all over town! And we've got one guy who *added* something."
"Added what?" I asked. "Well, he does like you said, stands staring at
them, gets them all upset and nervous, and then just before the elevator
doors close . . . he jumps *backward* off the elevator! Then, he runs up to the
next floor. And when the doors open, he tells them, 'I heard what you said
about me.'"

The technical term for such behavior is *elevator proxemics*, meaning
how people space themselves on elevators. In fact, *proxemics* is an
acknowledged area of study within psychology. There are kindred
branches as well. For example, *kinesics* is the study of body motion.
Kinesicists analyze body movements in slow motion. Anthropologists
have studied the kinesics of different cultures and substantiated that an
Arab, an Englishman, and a Latino signal to each other in notably different ways.

A pioneer researcher in kinesics is Ray Birdwhistell, but there are many other respected authorities. The British social anthropologist Desmond Morris gained considerable celebrity in 1967 with his book *The Naked Ape* (Jonathan Cape, London). In 1977, he produced the wonderfully illustrated and written hallmark book in this field, titled *Manwatching* (Abrams). We owe a great deal to Morris for his keen observations and dedicated research.

Another communications expert, Mario Pei, once estimated that humans can produce up to 700,000 different physical signs. Birdwhistell estimates that the face alone is capable of producing 250,000 expressions and reports that researcher M. H. Krout identified 5,000 distinct hand gestures that he believed had verbal equivalents while another researcher in kinesics, G. W. Hewes, has cataloged 1,000 different postures and their accompanying gestures.

How does verbal communication compare to nonverbal communication? Author George du Maurier once commented that "[The spoken] language is a poor thing. You fill your lungs with wind and shake a little slit in your throat, and make mouths, and that shakes the air; and the air shakes a pair of little drums in my head . . . and my brain seizes your meaning in the rough. What a roundabout way and what a waste of time."

Social scientist and author Flora Davis claims that gestures are shortcuts. They are much stronger than punctuation or the underscoring of words in boldface type or italics, she says. "They are like the maestro's baton to each musician in the ensemble."

Finally, *Time* magazine, in an essay written by Frank Trippett and titled "Why So Much Is Beyond Words," contends that "Homo sapiens, as a communicator, does not seem to have come all that far from the time when grunts and gesticulations were the main ways of getting messages across. Both individuals and groups still send vital messages by gesture, by pantomime, by dramatics—by a dizzy diversity of what scholars call nonverbal communications."

While any book on gestures and body signals would naturally draw from the science of kinesics, or nonverbal communications, this is not a scientific text. Instead, it deals only with the first thin layer of that science: the collection of gestures and body language floating on the surface of a culture. But it is precisely that assortment of signals a world wanderer first encounters as a tourist, a student, or a businessperson.

GESTURES ARE IMPORTANT

Gestures and body language have been called "the silent language." The collection of true stories that follows demonstrates how that "silence" has its own special volume—and its own direct impact on our lives.

- In 1988 in Los Angeles, an entertainer from Thailand was convicted of the second-degree murder of a twenty-nine-year-old Laotian. The entertainer was singing in an after-hours Thai cabaret when the Laotian, a patron, put his foot on a chair with the sole directed at the singer. When the cabaret closed, the entertainer followed the man and shot him. Why? Among Southeast Asians, showing or directing the sole of the shoe to another person is considered a grievous insult.

- In Nairobi, Kenya, in 1990, a ruling party boss urged his followers to chop off the fingers of people who flashed a two-fingered salute in support of permitting opposition parties. The leader told members of his party's youth wing this would discourage others from flashing the opposition's salute.

- In the fiercely conservative village of Muabda in southern Egypt, according to news reports in 1995, a wedding ceremony took place that resulted in two deaths and three people being wounded. Why? Because after the ceremony the groom took his bride's hand to lead her to their new home. It seems the brother of the bride became incensed by such a public display of affection. According to centuries-old traditions largely ignored today, the couple were not supposed to display any affection in public before the marriage was consummated. The brother therefore told the groom's uncle that his nephew was not raised properly. Tempers flared, guns appeared, and both the uncle and the brother died while three other guests were wounded in the melee. All because a married man and woman held hands.

- From acts of violence like the examples just mentioned, to the opposite end of the emotional spectrum—signs of love—our body actions are powerful signs. David Givens, author of *Love Signals* (Crown, 1983), claims that men and women unconsciously shrug their shoulders when they find each other attractive. Also, a woman attracted to a man will tilt her head down and to the side, then look in his direction in a coy or coquettish way. Let's look at some other examples.

- An American woman gets into a car with an American man, slides over to his side, and kisses him on the cheek. A common enough occurrence that probably happens hundreds of thousands of times each day in the United States. But in this case it happened in Saudi Arabia, where public displays of affection are disliked, even forbidden, and marriage is sacrosanct. The incident is reported by author Margaret K. Nydell, in her fascinating book *Understanding Arabs* (Intercultural Press, 1987). Nydell writes that the meeting between the man and woman happened to be seen by a captain of the Saudi National Guard who then demanded proof that the two were married. They were, but not to each other. "The woman was sent out of the country and the man, who compounded his problem by being argumentative, was sent to jail," Nydell writes.

- Just as love and affection can be signaled through actions and gestures, so can courage. A twelve-year-old American boy known as "David" was born without an immune system to shield him against disease. He lived his entire life inside a sterile plastic bubble and thus became known as "the bubble boy." It was not until the final fifteen days of his life when death was imminent that he emerged and, for the first time, experienced the touch of a hand unprotected by a glove, his mother's kiss, and the sensation of his mother running a comb through his long hair. As he lay dying he was conscious to the last. He made jokes and his final gesture, before he slipped into a sedated sleep that ended in death, was a wink at his doctor.

- Even the Queen of England has adopted special nonverbal signals. For example, you will probably never see her seated with her legs crossed *at the knees*. This is likely a vestige of Victorian days when "ladies" did not assume such a revealing posture. Instead, for English royalty, crossing the legs *at the ankles* is both proper and preferred.

- Queen Elizabeth II has also gone so far as to adopt certain body motions to signal messages to her entourage. Raymond Fullager, who writes and lectures about the royal family, claims Her Majesty uses *her purse* to send some twenty different signals to her staff. For example, when she shifts her handbag from her right arm to her left, it is a signal to her bodyguards to "Come and rescue me from this situation!"

- Winston Churchill is probably credited with putting the "V" for Victory sign in both our history books and our contemporary usage. During World War II, the picture of Churchill flashing the famous "V" became a familiar sight. In fact, it became a rallying point for the Allied forces against the Axis armies. So powerful was this gesture that even today statues can be seen of Churchill and his "V" frozen in time. (For a full account on the use of the "V" for Victory gesture, see pages 47–49).

- In 1995, Bill Richardson, a U.S. Congressman from New Mexico, traveled to Baghdad for an audience with Saddam Hussein to try to negotiate the release of two American men who had strayed into Iraqi territory and were retained for two months. Richardson shook hands with Hussein, sat down, and crossed his legs . . . whereupon Hussein rose abruptly and walked out of the room. Richardson had unwittingly insulted Hussein with his body language. In some Arab cultures, it is an offensive gesture to show the sole of one's shoe to another person because it is considered the lowest, dirtiest part of the body. Hussein later returned and the meeting resumed. Much later, the Americans were released, but it is correct to say Richardson had literally started negotiations off on the wrong foot.

- When American military forces were mobilized for the "Desert Shield" operation in Saudi Arabia, along with weapons, ammunition, and desert gear they packed a forty-page booklet on gestures and body language among the Arabs. For example, GIs were cautioned to refrain from gawking at Arab women and not even to consider trying to date them. Other tips: Don't be upset if Arabs stand very close, even touch you, when conversing; don't admire an Arab's possessions because he may then feel required to give you the object of your admiration as a gift on the spot. He also will expect a gift in return. Finally, the "O.K." gesture (thumb and forefinger forming a circle) may be interpreted there as giving a curse.

- Milton Neshek is an American lawyer and officer of a Japanese-owned company located in the North American Midwest. He once accompanied the governor of his state on a trade mission to Japan where the governor addressed a large and distinguished audience of Japanese officials. At the conclusion of the presentation, the visibly upset governor cornered Neshek and lamented, "My speech was a disaster! I shouldn't have delivered it. Why didn't my staff warn me?" Confused, Neshek asked, "What made you think it was so bad?" The governor complained he had seen many members of the audience asleep, even nodding their heads. Relieved, Neshek quickly explained that among the Japanese a common way to show concentration and attentiveness was to close the eyes in contemplation and nod the head slightly, up and down. What the governor read as boredom was actually a signal of respect and attention.

- The U.S. State Department recognizes the importance of bodily actions among other cultures. When I made my first business trip to the People's Republic of China in April 1976, our group was given a special briefing in Washington, D.C., because we were among the first businesspeople to travel to China after the détente arranged by President Nixon and Chairman Mao. Here are two relevant points extracted from that briefing:

— Chinese generally do not touch a drink at the dinner table without proposing a toast to others at the table, even if only by raising the glass and making eye contact. Only a symbolic sip need be taken in reply. It is perfectly acceptable to explain that one does not drink at all, providing one is consistent.

— Chinese are very sensitive to problems of precedence at doorways, in automobiles, and so on. Even a token gesture of yielding the right of way or the seat of honor to a Chinese is appreciated; failure to make the gesture when expected could be interpreted as arrogance.

- Eugene Theroux is a widely traveled international legal expert, having managed his law firm's offices in both the People's Republic of China and in the former USSR. "I was once startled," he writes, "in a negotiation in China to notice that the chief negotiator on the other side suddenly bent forward and began to press his temples with the two first fingers of each hand. I thought perhaps my negotiating style had driven him to the breaking point, until he smiled and explained that this is an acupressure technique for reducing stress." Theroux added, "And by the way, it works!"

- In commercial transactions, some Chinese buyers and sellers may be seen using an ancient, esoteric method of hand gestures to conduct business in secret. It is a secret bidding code. A buyer and seller will each place one hand under a cloth or some other cover. Then the bidder says only "hundred" or "thousand" out loud. Meanwhile, under the cloth, the bidder extends certain fingers of the hidden hand to indicate how many units he is bidding. If he says "thousand," and extends two fingers, that means 2,000; if he extends four fingers, it means 4,000, and so on.

- Author Helen Colton, in her book *The Gift of Touch* (Seaview/Putnam, 1983), graphically describes how different cultures react with varying gestures. In this case, she poses an embarrassing situation and tells how various people around the world would react. The situation: You suddenly come upon a strange woman in her bath. The varied reactions of that woman would be as follows:

— A Mohammedan woman would cover her face.

— A Laotian woman would cover her breasts.

— A Chinese woman (before the Revolution) would hide her feet.

— In Sumatra, the woman would conceal her knees.

— In Samoa, she would cover her navel.

— In the Western world, she would cover her breasts with one arm and her genital area with the other hand.[*]

- In 1968, the international sports world was shocked by a single arm and hand gesture. The scene appeared in photographs on newspaper front pages all over the world. At the 1968 Olympic games in Mexico City, two black Americans were strongly favored to win medals in the 200-meter race. Tommie Smith and John Carlos were students at San Jose State College and members of a group of athletes organized to protest the treatment of blacks in the United States. Smith won the gold and Carlos the bronze medal. At the medal awards ceremony, when the U.S. national anthem was played, spectators were stunned to see Smith and Carlos ascend the platform in bare feet, bow their heads, and raise one black-gloved hand in the Black Power salute. They later explained that their clenched fists symbolized black strength and unity and their bare feet signaled a reminder of black poverty in the United States. Their bowed heads, they said, signaled their belief that the words of freedom in the U.S. national anthem applied only to Americans with white skin. Their actions created a sensation and the U.S. Olympic Committee suspended the two athletes and commanded them to leave the Olympic village.

- At the end of many sporting contests in the United States and internationally, it is an act of good sportsmanship to shake hands with your opponents, right? Not always, it seems. At a California high school, baseball players were prohibited from shaking hands with their opponents for fear the ceremony would turn into fistfights. Some of the players were spitting on their hands before the handshake; some muttered insults; increasingly, some threw punches. Apparently it wasn't a game anymore.

- Virtually everywhere in the world clapping one's hands together in applause is a signal of honor, adulation, enjoyment, or approval. (Incidentally, you can detect whether a person is right-handed or left-handed by observing the way they applaud. A right-handed person will slap that hand down into and on top of the left palm; a left-handed person will make the left hand dominant.) In the United States,

---

[*]Excerpts reprinted by permission of the Putnam Publishing Group from *The Gift of Touch* by Helen Colton. Copyright © 1983 by Helen Colton.

clapping at large public events is often accompanied by whistling; however, in much of Europe, such whistling is a signal of derision and disapproval. In China, the customary way to greet visitors is with applause.

- How do the *deaf* signal applause? After all, they cannot hear the gratifying sound produced by applause. The answer is that they have adopted their own unique method of signaling enjoyment or approval. They raise their hands to shoulder or head height, palms outward, and shake them with a fast, almost shiveringlike motion. Seeing an audience waggling their hands in that fashion can be just as rewarding as hearing a thundering round of applause.

- One would naturally believe that conducting a philharmonic orchestra relied solely on one sense: hearing. But the conductor of the Buffalo, New York, Philharmonic Orchestra, interviewed on National Public Radio, explained that "Conducting is, in fact, a visual art. Through small gestures one influences the whole performance and its outcome."

- Some examples of gestures can seem almost amazing, even miraculous. Moments after being blessed by John Paul II at the Vatican, Jan Lavric, a visiting doctor from London, stunned bystanders by abruptly standing up, getting out of his wheelchair, and walking away. What appeared as a miracle was explained later by Lavric: "I was tired and sat down in an empty wheelchair. Suddenly, a nun wheeled me off, and before I could explain, the Pope blessed me."

- Gestures can also be a valuable form of opinion polling. According to *People* magazine, at least one U.S. politician had his own system of gauging his popularity. "I watch the crowds waving to me," he explained, "and I count the number of fingers they're using."

CONCLUSION

This book is intended to put you *en garde*—appropriately, a classic protective stance from the sport of fencing. As the global village continues to shrink and cultures collide, it is more and more essential for all of us to become *en garde*, figuratively speaking, to the myriad motions, gestures, and body language that surround us each day.

Another apt French expression is *beau geste*. It means, literally, a "beautiful gesture." It also served as the title of a well-remembered movie of the 1930s that related a heroic act of courage. It is an appropriate term for this book, and one worth remembering. As more of us cross over cultural borders, it would be our *beau geste* to learn, understand, and respect more about the silent but powerful language of gestures and body language.

The chapters that follow will help us do exactly that.

2

The Most
Popular Gestures

If there are, indeed, more than 700,000 different gestures that can be both powerful and contradictory, which gestures do we use the most?

In the 1970s, Desmond Morris (see Chapter 1) surveyed 1,200 informants in Western and southern Europe plus some Mediterranean areas and developed a list of what he called the twenty key gestures.

If I were to list some of those twenty—like "the fingers cross," "the eyelid pull," "the hand purse," and "the ear touch"—I doubt you would recognize them from those labels, much less categorize them as "most popular." By the time you finish this book, however, you will be able to recognize at least these twenty and understand their significance in a wide variety of cultures.

This chapter concentrates on four *general categories* of gestures:

- Greetings gestures

- Beckoning gestures

- Insulting gestures

- Touching gestures

and four *specific*, common, and popular gestures:

- "O.K." signal

- "Thumbs-up"

- "V" for Victory

- Vertical horns (or "hook 'em horns")

As you will see, just these eight types of popular gestures provide a dizzying variety of usages and meanings.

Among these eight groups of signals, you will quickly recognize a gesture and know its meaning . . . that is, the meaning according to *your* society, *your* geography, and *your* ethnic influences. The *other* interpretations from around the world for that same gesture should prove both informative and entertaining. In fact, knowledge of these varied interpretations might some day save you from a stern look, a strained relationship, or possibly even a smashed nose.

Example

An engineer for a New Jersey plastics machinery company relates this story. His firm purchased a German company in the same field and the two firms began exchanging engineers for purposes of product familiar-ization: One day, an American and German engineer were working side by side on a new machine. "Try increasing the pressure," the American suggested. The German did so, saying, "How is that? Did I do that cor-rectly?" The American replied by gesturing, making a circle with his thumb and forefinger, a sign used throughout North America to mean "O.K." The German abruptly put down his tools and walked away. He refused any further communication with the American. Finally, a super-visor forced the two men to sit down and reconstruct what happened. It seems that, to a German, when someone forms a thumb and forefinger in a circle, as the American had done, it signifies "You asshole."

To begin our study of popular gestures and how they can be misinter-preted depending on the country, we begin with the way most relation-ships begin: with the first handshake.

GREETINGS

Are greetings important? Consider this:

> *Item:* In January 1994, a simple handshake was the subject of great deliberation and discussion between two world leaders and U.S. president Bill Clinton. The occasion was the history-making accord between Palestinian leader Yasir Arafat and Israeli prime minister Yitzak Rabin. According to news reports, considerable discussion occurred over if, when, and how the two leaders should shake hands at the press announcement. Rabin was reti-cent, but Arafat was eager. Rabin reportedly agreed when Arafat assured him there would be no kissing of cheeks. Even then, via international television, the world witnessed as Arafat made the first move with his outstretched hand and Rabin exhibited momentary hesitation.

Like most of us, I learned the protocol of handshaking from my parents.
"When you shake hands," my father used to growl at me, "be sure you give 'em a good, firm grip. Also, look 'em straight in the eye."
Little did I realize that in other parts of the world fathers were teach-ing their sons and daughters something entirely different.
For example, fathers in India were instructing their children in the *namaste* (Figure 2.1), where the hands are placed in a praying position, about chest high, accompanied by a slight bow. With this gesture, you are saying, in effect, "I pray to the God in you." It also means "thank you" and "I'm sorry." In Thailand, this same gentle and gracious gesture is

**FIGURE 2.1   A man from India greeting
a Westerner with a *namaste.***

called the *wai.* Don't get carried away and lift the pressed hands above the head, however, or it could be construed as an insult.

The exact origins of both the handshake and *namaste* are unclear. Citizens of the Roman empire greeted each other with a hand-and-forearm clasp, but some anthropologists believe our handshake of today may be only a couple hundred years old.

Whatever the genesis, the intent seems clear. Whether it's the outstretched hand or the palms pressed together, each signal suggests openness and a clear sign that the greeter is not carrying a weapon.

Some believe the hug or embrace originally had a similar purpose: the assurance that no weapons were hidden beneath the flowing robes worn from the time of the Egyptians through the Middle Ages.

Another sign of openness when we greet one another involves the eyes and forehead. Anthropologists point out that when humans greet, regardless of our nationality or race, we all open our eyes wider than normal and wrinkle our foreheads. Since the eyebrows move upward, this is often referred to as the "eyebrow flash." Both motions appear to be instinctive and signal openness and are, therefore, a form of greeting.

There are other more exotic forms of greetings as well. In the Middle East, the older generation can still be seen giving the *salaam.* In this signal, the right hand sweeps upward, first touching the heart, then the forehead, and finally up and outward, perhaps with a slight nod of the head (Figure 2.2). The words that accompany this greeting are *salaam alaykum,* meaning, appropriately, "Peace be with you."

The Hollywood movie industry popularized the stereotype of a tall, bronze-skinned American Indian standing with palm upraised, saying "How." As every American schoolchild knows, that was the way all Native Americans greeted the palefaced settlers. At least that is what

FIGURE 2.2   The *salaam*, a Middle Eastern greeting.

Hollywood would have us believe. True or not, it is a fact that communication between different tribes of Native Americans and the first white explorers was solely through sign language. Therefore, the simple, raised palm as a form of greeting was critical to the exploration and opening of the U.S. West.

Greetings can also convey secret messages. On my last trip to the Mediterranean area, I was told that in many countries there, a greeting among homosexual men is to shake hands in a very specific and hidden manner: with the middle finger folded down into the palm.

Greetings can be downright physical, too, to the point you may want to wear a football helmet and shoulder pads. Eskimos greet each other by banging the other party with a hand either on the head or shoulders. Polynesian men who are strangers welcome each other by embracing and then rubbing each other's back.

The Maori tribespeople in New Zealand choose even today to greet each other with a gesture that seems to epitomize closeness and friendship: they rub noses (Figure 2.3). The Eskimos use this same gesture, but with more personal meaning.

Some East African tribes greet each other by spitting at each other's feet. And for perhaps the most unusual and mysterious greeting, Tibetan tribesmen are said to greet each other quite warmly by *sticking out their tongues* at each other.

Let's return to the more familiar gesture of greeting, the handshake. While *my* father was drilling me with "Firm handshake, direct eye contact," fathers in the Middle East were instructing their sons, "When you shake hands, a *gentle* grip is appropriate. Don't grip the hand firmly. A firm grip suggests aggression." And in places like Japan and Korea, fathers were not only advocating "Yes, gentle, not firm" but were adding "and try to avoid direct eye contact. Staring at someone is intimidating and disrespectful."

FIGURE 2.3   The Maori greeting.

Among North Americans and many Europeans, gripping a limp hand is distasteful. They liken it to being weak and effeminate. A simile often used is that it is like "grasping a dead fish."

Some people believe Americans go too far in the other direction, however. Prince Charles of England, who must be a connoisseur on greetings by now, has complained of the finger-crunching grip of the Americans. "Especially Texans," he adds.

Handshakes can be either "gentle," "firm," or "Texan." But there is more than just hand pressure involved in the business of shaking hands.

In northern Europe, you are most likely to receive a curt, firm, one-pump handshake. Also, women and children there will customarily extend their hand in greeting, whereas in parts of North America and in the Far East, women will only occasionally take that initiative. The same is true for children.

In Islamic countries, it is forbidden for unrelated men to touch women, so men should never offer to shake hands with women there. West African male friends will often add a snappy finish to a handshake as follows: as they release the grip, each middle finger is pressed together and then snapped abruptly into the fleshy pad below the thumb.

The French seem to be the most "handshakingest" of all. Visitors remark on how the French seem to shake hands when greeting, when departing, when returning . . . and repeat the custom each morning of every day, no matter if the relationship is business or social. Author Peter Mayle, in his engaging book *A Year in Provence* (Knopf, 1990), explains that if a Frenchman happens to have soiled hands he will offer his forearm in greeting, or if he is holding packages he will even extend a little finger to be grasped.

In South America, Bolivians win the title of "Greatest Greeters." Whenever two friends meet and chat, their greeting usually includes a handshake and a hearty clap on the back.

Psychologists regard the handshake as one of the most powerful of all tactile contacts, so maybe there's something to be learned from the French and the Bolivians.

In southern Europe and Central and South America, the handshake will usually be warmer and probably a bit longer, frequently accompanied by the left hand touching the other person's forearm, elbow, or even lapel.

A version popular in American politics is to shake hands using the free hand to cover the grip. On the scale of warmth of a greeting, this gesture supposedly adds several degrees of closeness and implied unity.

In Russia, good male friends, especially among the older generation, will start with a strong, firm handshake and then continue forward into the so-called bear hug so often identified with that country. But, just to demonstrate that common customs do not necessarily cross common boundaries, neighboring Finns firmly reject bear hugging. "Don't do it here," they warn. "We don't hug or kiss or have bodily contact with strangers as the Russians do."

In Latin American countries, the hug is called the *abrazo*, which means "embrace." It is often accompanied by a couple of hearty claps on the back (Figure 2.4). Most North Americans, northern Europeans, and Asians find any such touching or hugging very uncomfortable.

My first encounter with the Latin *abrazo* occurred in the airport at Buenos Aires, Argentina, when I was very new to this game of gestures and greetings. There to meet me, arms outstretched, was the manager of our local company. "My God," I thought, "that man is going to hug me!" My life seemed to pass before my eyes. Walking forward stiffly, I forgot that one must move the head either right or left. We ended up smashing noses.

Now let us turn to that most courtly of all greetings, the *bow*. Veteran travelers to Japan counsel, "When you visit Japan, keep your shoes shined at all times, since everyone will be looking at them a lot when

FIGURE 2.4 *Un abrazo* (embrace).

bowing." I am often asked, "Should a North American or European bow to a Japanese?" No, it is not absolutely necessary, but a slight bow demonstrates that you respect their customs. And in Japan, where style and grace and courteousness are revered, this simple act would surely be noted, appreciated, and probably remembered. Think about the subtle psychology of this and all gestures. Do we expect other cultures to adopt our customs, or are we willing to adopt theirs? This might translate to how business or even foreign relations are to be conducted. Do we compromise or force our associate to deal only on our terms? You may not have time to learn a language, but taking time to learn the "signals" can make you a powerful communicator.

Western businesspeople stationed in Japan know this and take pains to carefully emulate the Japanese. But they also joke among themselves: "You know you've stayed in Japan too long when you have a telephone conversation and find yourself bowing into the telephone." (See Figure 2.5.)

Many Westerners view the bow as an act of subservience, but in Japan that would be completely wrong. For the Japanese a bow signals respect and humility, two qualities coveted throughout Asia.

Westerners face many handicaps in trying to learn the complete art of Japanese bowing because there is so much hidden meaning in every dip and bob. For example:

- *Who bows first?*

- *How low does one bow?*

- *When do we shake hands?*

- *When do we exchange business cards?*

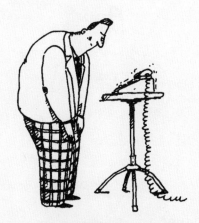

FIGURE 2.5

The answers are as follows:

Who bows first? And how low?

The operative word is *rank*. The shortcut for this lesson is simply to remember "The higher the rank of the person facing you, the lower you bow." In Japanese society, it is extremely important, especially in business, to know the rank of people with whom you come in contact. The same applies to the rank of your company. For example, the middle-level manager in a large powerful company outranks a department head from a smaller, less important company.

Therefore, who bows first and lowest? Answer: The person of lower rank bows first and lowest.

When do we shake hands?

The answer is complicated by the fact that many Japanese, especially those who travel abroad on business, are quickly adopting Western ways. As a result, our respective learning curves may collide midway. We may bow in respect to their practices, while they may simultaneously stick out their hand. They may even give a *firm* grip and add direct eye contact because they've been told that's how Westerners do it.

When do we exchange business cards?

Called *meishi* in Japanese, business cards are very important. The business card is more than a convenience. It represents one's personal identity, one's label, shingle, sign, rank, and name tag—all in one. (Incidentally, take care when listing your title on the card; make certain it is clear and accurate, neither overblown nor obscure. Also, have all the information printed in Japanese on the reverse side, preferably with the same quality printing on both sides lest you imply their language is second class.) In Japan, greetings and business cards go together like *sake* and rice. When exchanging business cards in Japan, the proper etiquette is:

- Exchange cards at the very first stages of an introduction.

- Present (and receive) the card with *both hands*. Grasp the card between thumbs and forefingers, with the lettering facing the recipient. Accompany all this with a slight bow. (See Figure 2.6.)

- Each recipient then takes several seconds to study the name, title, company name, and address before continuing.

- Now . . . shake hands and bow a few more times.

- Some final words of advice: Treat business cards with respect. The card is, after all, a symbol of that person's very identity. Avoid writ-

**FIGURE 2.6   In Japan, always present
and receive business cards with both hands.**

ing notes on it, at least in front of the other person. Avoid carrying
your cards or putting their card in your hip pocket—you are, obviously, then *sitting* on the cards. After receiving the other person's
card, place it respectfully on the table in front of you. And, speaking
of wrong signals, I've seen one bored American businessperson take
the Japanese person's card and absentmindedly *pick his teeth* with it!

In his informative book *Japanese Etiquette & Ethics in Business* (Passport
Books, 1987), author Boye DeMente advises, "The lower the bow and the
longer one holds the position, the stronger is the indication of respect,
gratitude, sincerity, obeisance, humility, contriteness, etc." DeMente
explains there are three degrees of bowing:

1. The informal bow (about 15 degrees, with the hands at the side),
   which is used for all casual occasions between people of all ranks;

2. The formal bow (30 degrees) with palms on knees, and often bobbing
   up and down; and

3. The formal or "highest form of salutation," which is rarely used and
   is reserved for the imperial family. (So we won't detail it here!)

As a final reminder of the importance of rank in Japan, they actually
joke among themselves that when playing golf it is customary to tee off
in accordance with the level of their respective salaries.

Elsewhere in Asia, in places like Taiwan, Hong Kong, Singapore, and
mainland China, the bow is much less common. In those places, the con-

ventional handshake is the customary form of greeting. You might detect a slight—very slight—bob of the head, but that's all.

Turning to other parts of the world, here are two more variations on the custom of shaking hands. In East Africa, friends shake hands with more of a casual light slap to each other's palm followed quickly by a cupping and grasping of fingers. And in Mexico, especially outside the metropolitan area of Mexico City, friends will greet with a conventional shaking of hands but then slip the palm upward and grasp each other's thumb.

A word of caution about the Thai *wai*, the Indian *namaste*, and Japanese bowing. While it is important to know, to practice, and to respect these forms of greetings, many people in the societies in which these greetings are practiced have traveled abroad and may have adopted the handshake as the lingua franca of physical greeting. Wherever you travel, the handshake may greet you. Nevertheless, be prepared to demonstrate your knowledge and respect for the local customs as well. This show of respect will be appreciated.

(There are "amplifiers" or extensions to this set of actions we call greetings. These will be discussed elsewhere in the book. For example, the whole subject of *kissing lips, cheeks,* and *hands* will be found in Chapters 3 and 4, under the appropriate sections on "lips" or "cheeks" or "hands.")

FAREWELLS

From greetings, we turn to *farewells.* The American good-bye wave can be interpreted in many parts of Europe and Latin America as the signal for "no." Cross-cultural misunderstandings work both ways: when Italians motion "good-bye," it can be interpreted by Americans as the gesture for "come here." Let's examine more of these cross-cultural good-byes.

FIGURE 2.7 The American good-bye.

FIGURE 2.8   The European good-bye.

Americans tend to wave good-bye with the hand up, palm out, wrist stiff, and with a back-and-forth motion with the whole forearm and hand. (See Figure 2.7.) It is sometimes described as a semaphore action. In much of Europe, that gesture does not mean "good-bye" but instead signifies "no."

In Europe, the customary way to wave "hello" or "good-bye" is with the arm up and extended out, with the palm down, and just the hand bobbing up and down at the wrist (Figure 2.8).

In direct contrast, Italians and Greeks will often wave good-bye with the arm extended, *palm up*, curling all the fingers back and forth toward themselves. Most Americans interpret that gesture as meaning "come here." (See Figure 2.9.) Greeting and beckoning have gotten completely twisted around.

FIGURE 2.9   The Italian and Greek good-bye.

The Vulcan gesture from *Star Trek*.

We conclude this section on farewells with one from television land. Leonard Nimoy, the actor who played Mr. Spock, the pointy-eared Vulcan space alien in the long-running series *Star Trek*, was asked to create a gesture to accompany the Vulcan farewell: "Live long and prosper." The gesture he came up with—hand lifted, palm out, with the fingers separated into a **V** shape—is a Jewish priestly benediction he recalled having seen in synagogues, where its significance is that it resembles the Hebrew letter that is the first letter of a word that represents God's name.

BECKONING

We now turn to the second group of common gestures—*beckoning gestures*. The way people beckon one another around the world can be almost as diverse as the way we greet and bid farewell to one another. (See Figure 2.10.)

FIGURE 2.10   Beckoning.

Think about this commonplace situation for a moment: If you are seated in a restaurant and you wish to attract the attention of the waiter or waitress, what do you do? The odds are that whatever gesture you customarily use may be interpreted as strange or even rude in some other part of the globe.

In the following discussion, we review a series of common beckoning gestures and where they are popular, along with explanations of *other* meanings each gesture may have in other parts of the world.

In the United States, the common gesture for getting someone's attention, as when calling a waiter, is to raise a hand (with the index finger raised) about head high, or a little higher (Figure 2.11). It probably stems from our first experiences in school, where we are taught simply to raise our hand in order to get the teacher's attention. There are many variations.

The gesture in Figure 2.11 could be considered rude in some countries, like Japan, where pointing the finger at anyone is considered impolite.

In places like Germany, the signal as shown in Figure 2.11 also means "two," because two fingers (one finger and a thumb) are being held upright. So an American might be signaling in this fashion and then saying "Waiter—some water, please," and a German waiter would bring two glasses of water.

Another beckoning or attention-getting motion common in the United States is simply to raise the hand and with the full, open palm wave the hand back and forth to attract attention.

The trouble with this motion is that in, say, Europe it could be interpreted as signaling "no." So, an American could be trying to get the attention of the waiter to come to his table and the waiter, seeing the gesture, says to himself: "That fellow is signaling 'no' to me. I guess he doesn't need me."

**FIGURE 2.11 The most common
beckoning gesture in the United States.**

Also in America, a person might curl the index finger in and out to signal "come here."

In countries as widespread as the former Yugoslavia and Malaysia, that gesture is used only for calling *animals*. Therefore, using it to beckon a human would be terribly impolite.

In Indonesia and Australia, it is also used for beckoning "ladies of the night."

Throughout much of Europe and in many Latin American countries the preferred gesture for signaling "come over here" is to extend the arm, hand out, palm down, and then make a scratching motion with the fingers (Figure 2.12).

North Americans do not customarily use this gesture and may consider it uncomfortable, effeminate, or puzzling.

If not done properly, in some European countries, particularly Italy and Greece, this gesture might be confused with one used to signal "good-bye." In that case, though, while the palm faces down, the fingers are *waggled* up and down as opposed to making an inward, scratching motion.

In France, the preferred way to call a waiter to your table is simply to catch his eye and then perhaps nod the head backward quickly.

In Colombia, one way to get a waiter's attention is to clap the hands lightly.

FIGURE 2.12   A beckoning gesture used in many European and Latin American countries.

In China, to beckon a waiter to refill your tea, simply turn your empty cup upside down in its saucer. If the teapot is empty, turn its lid upside down. These gestures have no significance at all in most other countries.

In Spain, Mexico, Haiti, and a sprinkling of other countries, when calling a waiter, restaurant patrons can be heard issuing a noise with the lips, something like "hssssst," or "pssssst." Another variation is to *snap the fingers*. But guidebooks caution that while this may be done by some local inhabitants, it is often considered impolite if done by visitors.

On one of my visits to Brazil, my group was seated in a fine restaurant with waiters scurrying busily around us, so I used the opportunity to ask my dinner companions, "What is the preferred way to get a waiter's attention in Brazil?" "Oh, we don't ever gesture or signal to get a waiter's attention," was the answer of my rather refined host. "In a fine restaurant, you should never have to call the waiter—he should hover so closely near your side that all you have to do is raise your head upward and whisper your wishes."

In Mexico I discovered perhaps a most unique way of beckoning a waiter. In some parts of the country they purse and pucker the lips and make a kissing noise with the lips. I would, however, in other countries urge you to exercise extreme caution in using this signal!

Try using this category of gestures to start your own investigation of various signals around the world. When you are visiting another country and being hosted by local nationals at dinner, just ask, "What is the customary way to beckon a waiter here?" It is an easy way to slip into a discussion of different gestures used around the world. And you may even discover a new beckoning gesture.

We now turn to the most delicate territory of all in the field of signals around the world: insulting gestures.

INSULTING GESTURES

When it comes to flashing nonverbal *insults*, humans are clear, colorful, and creative—but sometimes contradictory.

Insulting gestures can be especially confusing because, as evidenced earlier in the incident between the American and German plastics engineers, some gestures you would use freely in front of your stodgy American Aunt Wilma would fry the hair of, say, your European Aunt Marie.

The award for the most ubiquitous and longest-lived insulting gesture goes, as you may have suspected, to *The Finger*, hand down (pun intended). This gesture is performed by holding up the fist, knuckles facing outward, and extending the middle finger upward stiffly. It can simply be a static, frozen gesture, or it can be accompanied by a thrusting or jerking motion upward (Figure 2.13).

FIGURE 2.13 *Digitus impudicus.*

Item: Associated Press, September 3, 1993— "A brawl among motorists on Interstate 43 [near Waukesha, Wisconsin] was started by an exchange of obscene hand gestures and left a smashed windshield and a passenger with a broken nose."

Item: In July 1995, Jack McDowell, right-handed baseball pitcher for the New York Yankees, created a scandal when he left a game amid boos and heckles and responded by raising his middle finger in the air and twirling it for emphasis. He later admitted, "It was a stupid thing to do," but nonetheless a photo of him performing the gesture appeared in newspapers across the country and he was fined $5,000 by the club's management.

Regardless of how this "single-digit salute" is used, it sends a powerful insulting message with little room for misunderstanding. And it has been that way for centuries. According to anthropologists, this gesture has been used for over 2,000 years. The Romans even had a special name for it, calling it *digitus impudicus* in Latin, or "indecent digit." Morris writes that "The [Roman] Emperor Caligula is thought to have used the extended middle finger when offering his hand to be kissed, as a deliberately scandalous act."

If Caligula were reincarnated to modern-day California, he could drive the highways there and instantly recognize that very same "scandalous" gesture. There it is sometimes called "the expressway digit" and used when an impatient, irate driver wishes to signal anger and frustration to another driver.

Arabs have modified this gesture in a peculiar way. For them the same insult is conveyed by extending the hand, palm down, fingers splayed outward, with the middle digit directed straight down (Figure 2.14).

FIGURE 2.14 The Arab version of "The Finger."

The Russians also have a variation. According to Tad Tuleja in his entertaining book *Curious Customs* (Stonesong Press, 1987), the Russians bend back the middle finger of one hand with the forefinger of the other hand. It's called "looking under the cat's tail," a term that sounds as uninviting as it is rude.

Whether held up or down, the extended middle digit is generally regarded as a phallic symbol. In American slang, it sends a very strong and clear message. Another American label for this gesture is, curiously, "the bird," as in the expression "So I flipped him the bird."

While the indecent digit is usually displayed openly and forcefully, it has also been used at least once to send a historic cryptic message. In 1968 the U.S. Navy ship *Pueblo* was captured by North Koreans and the American crew held captive for many months. During their imprisonment, a photograph was taken of the crew and circulated by the North Koreans to show that the sailors were in good health. When the photo was taken, one of the crew surreptitiously displayed "the finger" in an attempt to signal defiance and indicate that the photo was a staged, insulting situation. The American press revealed this, and when the North Koreans learned of it, they severely punished the offender.

An enlarged version of the middle finger jerk is the *forearm jerk*, also called "the banana" in Brazil. Morris classifies this powerful and well-known gesture as a phallic symbol used mainly by men (Figure 2.15).

Again, the message is strong, sexual, and insulting. In American street lingo, it is yet another way to signal "Up yours!"

When issuing this gesture, there are several variations or levels of intensity. For example, in the former Yugoslavia a man may simply bend the arm at the elbow, make a fist (with knuckles away from his face), and shake the fist once (Figure 2.16). When I asked my guide in Dubrovnik,

FIGURE 2.15   The forearm jerk.

"Exactly what does that gesture mean?" he looked at me, startled, and replied, "What does it exactly mean?? It exactly means f—k you!"

In North America, Latin America, and many parts of Europe, the forearm jerk is done using *both* arms in a clearly dynamic action: The right arm is bent at the elbow and the left hand then comes chopping down into the crook of the elbow while the fist of the right hand is jerked upward. For even greater emphasis and intensity, the left hand can also slap the *shoulder* of the right arm (Figure 2.17).

Next on any listing of widespread and well-known insulting gestures might come a grouping called "animal insults." As a child, you probably used two of them to mock or taunt another child. They are the "ear waggle" and the "thumbing of the nose."

**FIGURE 2.16   The forearm jerk in
countries of the former Yugoslavia.**

FIGURE 2.17 Forearm jerk, with emphasis!

With the *ear waggle* (Figure 2.18), the person places the hands at either side of the head, thumbs pointing inward at the temples or ears, and the other fingers spread. When one does this and flaps the hands back and forth, he is probably imitating the long, floppy ears of the donkey, an animal usually depicted as lazy and stupid.

Thumbing the nose involves placing the thumb of one hand on the tip of the nose with the other fingers splayed outward and then making a wiggling motion (Figure 2.19). Morris believes "This is thought to represent the hostile, erect comb of a fighting cock." There is another possible explanation, he says, and that is that it "relates to the ancient practice of imitating grotesque, long-nosed effigies."

While we seem to have a whole kaleidoscope of derisive gestures all over the world, these two are not only universally known but frequently

FIGURE 2.18 The ear waggle.

FIGURE 2.19 Thumbing the nose.

used by young children everywhere. What swift, underground communication system causes them to learn these gestures at such an early age?

In contrast to the more universal insulting gestures used by many cultures, here are some specific, unique insulting gestures from individual countries.

- In France, if you play an imaginary flute, you are sending a signal saying, "You are talking so long, I am getting bored."

- In Syria, picking the nose is a graphic signal to indicate "Go to hell!"

- In the United States, if a person imitates the action of shoveling, he is saying, "This person (who is speaking) is creating a lot of manure."

- Among Jewish people, if one person points to his palm he is saying, in effect, "Grass will grow on my palm before what I am hearing comes true."

Gestures for indicating that *someone*—or something—*is crazy* are legion. In the United States, one twirls the forefinger around the area of the temple or ear (which, in Argentina, could be misinterpreted to mean "You have a telephone call").

In Germany, motorists who drive crazily may see nearby motorists put their forefingers to their temples and rotate them back and forth. So strong is this message and so insulting that one can possibly be arrested for it.

In Italy, whenever you see Italians tapping their hands to their forehead in a saluting manner, they are probably signaling the message that "You're *pazzo* (crazy)."

And take special care in Holland, where tapping the *temple* with the forefinger means someone is intelligent. But to indicate someone is considered stupid, the Dutch will tap the *forehead*. What a difference six inches can make.

One insulting gesture started one of the theater's best-known feuds. Here's the story.

In Elizabethan times, it was considered an insult to make a fist, place the thumbnail against the teeth, and then flick outward. William Shakespeare used this gesture in *Romeo and Juliet*, Act I, scene I. When Sampson of the Capulet family flicks his thumb in this manner at Abram of the house of Montague, the Bard wrote "which is disgrace to them if they bear it." The Montagues reply with, "Do you bite your thumb at us, sir?" and sword fighting ensues.

Another insulting gesture with deep historic roots is the *moutza* of Greece. This is known as the *hand push*. At first glance, it merely looks like the person is holding his palm out toward you, as a traffic policeman might do to signal "Stop!" It is often accompanied by closing one eye and placing the other hand on the knee.

The *moutza* reaches back into ancient Greek history when fecal matter and dirt were hurled or pushed into the face of war prisoners. As a signal of insult, it survives with important implications even today. (See Figure 2.20.) A Western tourist visiting Greece might casually reject a vendor's plea with the hand, palm up and outward, and unknowingly be using an ugly signal as old as the Acropolis. And in West Africa this gesture means "You could have any one of five fathers!" which is another way of calling a person a bastard.

Two other widespread insulting gestures involve the fist and the tongue. The *fist* gesture is a curious action because done one way, with the knuckles facing outward, it is a combative, threatening, and aggressive gesture.

Figure 2.20 The Greek *moutza*.

But, if the fist is rotated so the gathered fingers are displayed outward, it converts into a gesture of pride, power, or victory.

The upraised fist, with the fingers outward, has become synonymous with the Black Power movement. History books show three separate scenes where this gesture has become memorialized: U.S. sprinter Tommie Smith at the 1968 Olympics in Mexico; Martin Luther King during his many protest marches; and Nelson Mandela of South Africa on his triumphant 1990 tour of the United States and Europe. Each helped implant the concept of Black Power in the minds of the world.

Yet, with a mere 180-degree rotation of the forearm, wrist, and hand, that fist gesture appears in the same history books with pictures showing rebellious crowds and angry demonstrators shaking their fists in unquestioned bellicosity.

Finally, let us turn to an assortment of what are considered ordinary, bland gestures in one society but which are insulting in others.

You will read more detail about each of these in pages that follow, so descriptions here will be brief:

- The "O.K." sign is terribly rude, even insulting, in diverse places like Russia, Germany, and Brazil. And, as you will learn later, in places like France and Japan it has entirely different meanings.

- The popular "V" for Victory gesture, *in reverse* could lead to painful consequences.

- The "vertical horns" gesture has a mixture of meanings, and one of them—in Italy—is very insulting.

- The "fig" gesture is an expression of good luck in Brazil but is terribly rude in Turkey.

- Even the "thumbs-up" gesture is derogatory in some countries (e.g., Australia, Nigeria).

As a final demonstration of just how casual, innocent gestures in one society can actually be crude and insulting in another, imagine this scene:

You are standing on a street corner, hands free of bundles or briefcases, whiling away the time in a free and happy mood. You swing your arms a bit, and casually smack the fist of one hand into the palm of the other. If you happen to be in a place like Chile or France, you have just flashed to all those around you the equivalent of "Up yours!" (See Figure 2.21.)

FIGURE 2.21 The "innocent abroad," cheerful on a sunny afternoon, casually gestures, "Up yours!"

Often, when I relate this story, people react by saying, "From now on, I'm just going to travel the world with my hands in my pockets." But in Japan, France, Belgium, and a sprinkling of other countries, standing with your hands in your pockets can be considered impolite.

The final general category of most popular gestures and body language might appropriately be called "The touchy subject of *touching*."

TOUCHING

On my first trip to the Middle East, my Arab business contact and I toured the city, walking along the street visiting customers. He wore his long robe, the air was hot and dusty, a muezzin chanted the call to prayers from a nearby minaret, and I felt as far away from my American home as one could possibly be. At that moment, my business friend reached over, took my hand in his, and we continued walking along, his hand holding mine.

It didn't take me long to realize that something untoward was happening here, that some form of communication was being issued . . . but I didn't have the faintest idea what that message was. Also, I suddenly felt even farther from home.

Probably because I was so stunned, the one thing I didn't do was pull my hand away. I later learned that if I had jerked my hand out of his, I could have committed a Sahara-size *faux pas*. In his country, this act of taking my hand in his was a sign of great friendship and respect.

That was my first lesson about spatial relationships between different people. I quickly learned that it was a world of extremes—important extremes—with some cultures seeking bodily contact and others studiously avoiding it. Ken Cooper, in his book *Nonverbal Communication for Business Success* (AMACOM, 1979), writes that he once covertly observed conversations in outdoor cafes in several different countries and counted the number of casual touches (of self or of the other party) per hour. The results: San Juan, Puerto Rico, 180 per hour; Paris, 110 per hour; Florida, 2 per hour; London, 0 per hour.

I also learned that the Middle East was not the only region where it is quite acceptable for two men to walk cradling an elbow, arm-in-arm, or even holding hands. Korea, Indochina, Greece, and Italy are also regarded as "touch-oriented" countries. Such physical displays in those countries usually signal friendship. Touching between men—often seen as an indication of homosexuality in North America—is quite the opposite. In some of the most "touch-oriented" areas, homosexuality is coldly rejected.

Here, on a scale of "touch" or "don't touch," is a geographic measuring stick:

Touch	Don't Touch	Middle Ground
Middle East countries	Japan	France
Latin American	United States	China
countries	& Canada	Ireland
Italy	England	India
Greece	Scandinavia	
Spain & Portugal	Other northern	
Some Asian countries	European countries	
Russia	Australia	
	Estonia	

Can the casual act of touching be all that important? The answer is yes—important enough to make bold headlines in at least one country's national newspapers:

> When Queen Elizabeth paid one of her periodic visits to Canada, a Canadian provincial transport minister escorted her through a crowd by gently touching her elbow; he may have even touched the small of her back. Newspaper headlines in England screamed protests: "Hands off our Queen," said one; "Row Over Man Who Touched Queen," read another.

The reason behind that uproar was that it is an unwritten rule among the British that no one touches the Queen. Even when shaking hands, the rule is that she must make the first move.

In the United States, office workers and schoolteachers are warned and trained to avoid any casual touching of their employees or students. A university professor of communications explains that "an innocuous touch on someone's hand or arm can be misconstrued as a sexual move, especially if we let it linger." Unwanted touching in U.S. business offices can lead to lawsuits for sexual harassment while teachers may be accused of molestation if they frequently hug, pat, or touch their students.

Yet there are strange contradictions, especially in the United States. Here are two examples:

I once asked an audience of U.S. businessmen what they would do if they boarded a crowded airplane, sat next to a large man, and found themselves pressing elbows, maybe even shoulders and upper arms as well, throughout the whole trip. "Nothing," was the consensus. "It happens all the time," they agreed. I countered, "Well, what would you do then if that same man then touched your knee with his hand?" The reaction was unanimous: "Move the knee." "And," one added, "if, God forbid, he *grabbed* my knee, I would punch him in the nose."

The second contradiction regarding rules for touching, occurs on elevators and subways. As we learned in Chapter 1, on a crowded elevator or an underground train at commuting time, people will stand shoulder-to-shoulder, arm-to-arm, and accept such rubbing of shoulders without complaint. But the rule is, "Touch *only* from shoulder to elbow. No other parts of the body."

Cultures are colliding every day over this dilemma of "to touch or not to touch." In New York City, Korean immigrants in recent years have started new lives by opening retail shops of all kinds. But when American customers make a purchase and receive their change, the Korean merchants place the money on the counter to avoid any physical contact. "They won't touch my hand," one customer noticed. "They won't even place coins in my hand. It's somewhat cold and insulting. And furthermore, they won't look me in the eyes."

One Korean merchant explained in a national television interview that in his homeland they are taught to avoid physical contact of any kind. The same with direct eye contact. "We are taught that either gesture could have sexual connotations," he added, "so we carefully avoid them."

And here's a surefire way for a North American to make a Japanese acquaintance feel uncomfortable. Just go up and place your arm around him, as you would a college buddy or big brother. Even though the Japanese permit themselves to be jammed into subways and trains, they are not regarded as a touching society. To explain this, anthropologist Edward T. Hall says the Japanese handle any unease about being packed into public places by averting eyes, avoiding eye contact, drawing within themselves, and thus "touching without feeling."

Closely related to the societal customs of touching is that of spatial relationships. Anthropologists tell us that each of us walks around inside "bubbles of personal space." The size of the bubble represents our personal territory, territorial imperative, or "personal buffer zones." We neither like nor tolerate it when someone invades our bubble. We become distinctly uncomfortable.

But as we travel to different places around the world, we learn that some cultural bubbles are larger or smaller than others. Here is a ruler for measuring the bubbles between nationalities:

- The American "bubble" extends about 12 to 15 inches, and so we may stand a combined 24 to 30 inches apart. Scientists point out this just happens to be an arm's length away (which carries a certain symbolism, doesn't it?). Anthropologist George Renwick says, "When two Americans stand facing one another in any normal social or business situation, one could stretch out his arm and put his thumb in the other person's ear."

- Asians, and especially the Japanese, stand even farther apart, Renwick adds. When it comes to ordinary business or social situations, they have the largest bubbles of all. However, as we have learned, in their own public settings, where crowding is impossible to avoid, they accept body contact or just seem to ignore it by "retreating within themselves."

- Latins and Middle Easterners, on the other hand, stand much closer than Americans. They may stand, literally, toe-to-toe. They may even place a hand on the other's forearm or elbow, or finger the lapel of the other person.

Americans claim it takes years of experience, plus steely resolve, to stand that close and smell that many breaths. Some observers in Latin America even have a name for this charade. They call it "the conversational tango." That's the "dance" done by an American or European freshly arrived in Latin America who is confronted by this sudden and startling custom of closeness. The first reaction of the visitor is to step backward. But the Latin will follow. So, the visitor steps back again. The Latin follows. And so it goes, in a poorly choreographed tango (Figure 2.22). As one observer put it, "The dance stops only when the American is backed into a corner."

But even as these words are written, touch codes are changing all over the world. In the United States, politicians have learned the value of touch. They frequently give two-handed handshakes, casually touch the elbow of another, or lightly touch the back of the person standing next to them. "Pressing flesh" has become a byword on political campaigns.

FIGURE 2.22 The first step in a conversational tango.

Also, Japanese managers posted to U.S. factories are steeling themselves and learning to accept finger-crunching handshakes, back patting, and maybe even a friendly arm around the shoulder for the softball team photo.

The "hugging professor," Leo Buscaglia, tours cities and campuses presenting captivating lectures on the joy of hugging. His popular books and video and audio tapes make his audiences realize that separateness and aloofness can be a lonely, cold existence.

Finally, in Helen Colton's wonderful book, *The Gift of Touch*, she describes how Swedish actress Liv Ullmann was once touring famine-stricken lands on behalf of UNICEF. In Bangladesh, after a warm visit with a woman there, Ullmann gave the woman a hug. But she felt the woman suddenly draw away. Through her interpreter, Ullmann asked why. The woman answered, "In my country, we kiss feet when we say good-bye." Ullmann, the quintessential lady, unhesitatingly bent down and kissed the woman's feet. Then they hugged, each woman having exchanged the parting ritual of her own world.

We now turn to four specific and common gestures. Each of these is used and known in a large number of societies—but, as you will see, each gesture has different meanings attached to it depending on the locale.

THE "O.K." SIGN

In the 1950s, then–Vice President Richard Nixon made a goodwill tour of Latin America. At that time, there was already widespread hostility toward the United States and Nixon unwittingly added fuel to the fires of resentment with a single, unthinking act. At one of his early stops, Nixon

FIGURE 2.23

stepped off his airplane and flashed the "A-O.K." sign to the waiting crowd. They responded by booing. In addition, newspapers the next day published large photographs of Nixon and his gesture. Why was it headline news? Because in their culture, what Nixon had signaled was the gesture equivalent for "You asshole!" (See Figure 2.23.)

A Frenchman, particularly in the south of France, would read that very same gesture as meaning "zero" or "worthless." I once took a hotel room in France and when the concierge asked "Is your room satisfactory?" I replied with the "O.K." sign. With a shrug of irritation, the concierge said, "If you don't like it, we'll just have to find you another room."

In Japan, the thumb and forefinger making a circle is used as a symbol for money—the fingers creating the round outline of a coin. For example, when a Japanese buys a newspaper or soft drink and wants the change in coins, he or she might flash this gesture.

Because of this use, the gesture could have serious consequences when incorrectly used. Imagine a Western businessperson who has negotiated a contract with a Japanese and, at the conclusion, casually makes the "O.K." sign and says: "Fine. Let's sign the contract." The Japanese might say to himself, "Oh! He's giving me the sign for 'money.' Is he saying he wants some money to sign? Is he asking for a bribe?"

The connections between this gesture and coins, zero, and anatomy are clearer than how and why this gesture means "O.K." In American Sign Language for the deaf, the thumb-and-finger-circle designates the letter O, but the other three fingers on the hand are cupped as well. Also, the letter K is made by making a "V" with the index and middle fingers. So, our "O.K." sign apparently does not come from that source.

The spoken term for "O.K." probably originated in the United States in 1840. At that time, the Democratic party's "Old Kinderhook" label was given to its presidential candidate Martin Van Buren, who was born in Kinderhook, New York. As a campaign slogan, this was shortened to "O.K. Van Buren." One supposition might be that the circle signals the letter *O* and the other three outstretched fingers are a crude replica of the letter *K*, but the exact origin is unclear.

A very crude variation on this gesture is to form a circle with the thumb and forefinger of one hand and then poke the forefinger of the other hand through the circle. In many locales, this is considered an obscene way to signal the act of coitus.

Clearly, the "O.K." gesture as Americans and many others know it, is "non-O.K." when landing in other lands and communicating among other cultures. Better, perhaps, to quickly learn the words in the local language for "Yes" and "Fine" and keep your hands at your side.

THUMBS-UP GESTURE

Pilots do it the world over. Astronauts and cosmonauts even do it out of this world. It has become an almost universal signal for "everything's O.K." or "fine" or "good going!" and a dozen other messages along that vein.

But watch out! There are some exceptions—important exceptions. Before we get to those, however, let's review the origins of the gesture.

Origins, according to Hollywood's portrayal, go back to the gladiators of Rome who received the "thumbs-up" signal from the emperor who thought that a courageous gladiator should live, or "thumbs-down," which signaled the opposite, a bloody death sentence for the losing warrior.

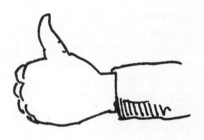

Once again, Hollywood may be guilty of creating its own history.

Desmond Morris suggests that there are no ancient references to this symbol. He contends that recent historians may have misunderstood the Latin phrase *pollice verso* to mean a "downturned thumb." That bit of Latin means instead, according to him, "a turned thumb," one that is moved in some unspecified way. No direction was specified. Morris theorizes that the ancient Romans would extend their thumbs in some fash-

**FIGURE 2.24   The "innocent abroad" in Australia
tries to close the deal . . . with "Up yours!"**

ion when they wished to signal death. Furthermore, he contends that to
signal "he shall live," they would tuck their thumb inside their fist.

Whatever the origin—Hollywood or history—the thumbs-up gesture
is now well known throughout North America and much of Europe. It is
perhaps least known in Greece and Italy, but even there it has been
imported and observed (although not widely). The same is true in the Far
East where it is largely imported and known as a Western gesture.

In the United States and parts of Europe, the thumbs-up gesture is
commonly used to signal that one is hitchhiking. In Nigeria, however, as
we learned in an incident related in Chapter 1, it is viewed as a rude gesture. Foreigners traveling in Nigeria have innocently tried hitchhiking
only to be roughed up for appearing to be sending insults to passing
motorists.

In the "down under" country, posing the thumbs-up gesture might
just get you "down and out." In Australia, flashing the upright thumb
and then making a slight jerk upward is generally used to silently signal
"Up yours!" (See Figure 2.24.)

If you like *counting* with your fingers, be cautious as you travel
abroad because you might just add up to total confusion. In Germany, for
example, to signal "one," a person uses the upright thumb instead of the
forefinger. Therefore, in a German *gasthaus* beer garden, to order "one
beer" you would flash the thumbs-up gesture. Many Westerners use the
forefinger to signal "one," more or less ignoring the thumb. But, do that in

Germany—casually hold up the forefinger and forget the thumb—and it could be seen as meaning "two," with the result that you'd be drinking two beers instead of one.

In Japan, they use the fingers to count visually just as most cultures do. However, in Japan, counting *begins* with the index finger (not the thumb) to designate "one"; then the index and middle fingers combined equal "two"; the combination of index, middle, and ring fingers is "three," and adding the little finger equals "four." Then the Japanese show the upright thumb alone to mean "five." So, if you order "one beer" with your thumb in Japan, you may well receive five beers.

When one thinks about it, the thumb is a wonderfully versatile and utilitarian digit. Artists hold it in front of their eyes, peering over it to gain a sense of perspective and depth. We like to put people "under our thumb," and film critics and editorial writers frequently use "thumbs-up" or "thumbs-down" to indicate approval or rejection, respectively. Finally, we "thumb our noses," bite our thumb to hurl an insult à la Shakespeare, suck our thumbs as infants, and if that is not sufficient, there must be at least a million "rules of thumb."

So the thumb becomes a valuable part of our daily worldwide communication, whether in school to ridicule a schoolmate with the "nose thumb" or in space to reassure a spacemate with the thumbs-up gesture.

Just be careful where you point your thumb in places like Nigeria and Australia.

"V" FOR VICTORY

Since World War II, followed by the Peace Movement of the 1960s, holding two fingers upright has signaled "victory" or "peace" for millions of people.

But in England, where it probably originated, an innocent twist of the wrist could result in a jolt in the nose. There, if the *palm and fingers face inward*, it means "Up yours!" especially if executed with an upward jerk of the fingers (Figure 2.25).

I once had the pleasure of appearing on the Merv Griffin late-night television show. I demonstrated that "V" for Victory flashed with the fingers and palm *outward* was fine. But then I asked Griffin, "But in England do you know what it means if you turn the hand around?" "Oh, I bet I know," Griffin said quickly. "It's like 'the finger' only *double*. It's like saying 'And here's one for your mother, too!' "

A more plausible story about the origin of the rude version of this gesture was supplied to me by a military historian in England. Five hundred years ago, English bowmen were considered as destructive as today's nuclear weapons. Consequently, if such a bowman were cap-

**FIGURE 2.25 The "innocent abroad"
befriends a Britisher . . . with "Up yours!"**

tured, the French reportedly cut off the forefinger and middle finger of the hand that drew the bowstring. That had the effect of disarming the English archer for life.

After the battles of Agincourt and Crécy, so the story goes, where the French were heavily defeated by the expert English archers, the surviving French were marched off the battlefield to the taunts of the victorious English. The English added further insult to the French by holding up their hands, forefinger and middle finger stiffly upright, palms inward, to show both fingers fully intact.

Winston Churchill may have known this historic tidbit because he adopted the "V" as a courageous gesture in World War II. It became so identified with him that contemporary statues and history books frequently show him proudly displaying that gesture. But, we should note, with the palm facing *outward*, and therefore not the insult the English bowmen flashed at the French.

Other historians might argue that Churchill adopted that signal only after a Belgian radio announcer, Victor De Lavelaye, popularized the opening notes of Beethoven's Fifth Symphony, which in Morse code was the signal for the letter *V*. Thus, according to this version, the *sound* came first, then the "V" in Morse code, and *then* Churchill adopted it as his visual signature.

Today French, Americans, and other nationalities are seen presenting the "V" for Victory or Peace signal . . . but unknowingly flashing it *either* way, palm out or palm in. Most are not aware that when visiting England one of those versions could very possibly result in a reaction far removed from "peace." In fact, the result might possibly be an English bloody, bloody nose.

Even former president George Bush has provided a quip on the various origins and meanings of the "V" signal. While jogging one morning, according to news reports, he flashed the "V" signal and mischievously asked journalists accompanying him, "Do you know what this means? It's Julius Caesar ordering five beers."

Bush wasn't as clever during a visit to Australia in 1991. While riding in his limousine in the streets of Sydney, he signaled what he *thought* was "V" for Victory to the crowds lining his route. Unfortunately, his palm was facing the wrong way, and an alert news photographer captured his gaffe for that day's editions, much to the chagrin of millions of Aussies.

Finally, just when we believe we have correctly divined all of the various meanings of a particular gesture, we can be wrong. Visiting the island of Madeira in 1995, I quizzed our guide, Louisa, about common hand gestures in use there. Since Madeira is Portuguese, I knew that the "O.K." sign was considered rude, and the thumbs-up gesture was acceptable. But when I did this, the "V" sign, Louisa looked at me strangely. "You want to know what that means?" she asked somewhat incredulously. Thinking I had stumbled on to some forbidden territory, I paused. But Louisa continued: "Why it's simple. That means 'two.' "

VERTICAL HORNS, OR "HOOK 'EM HORNS"

For thousands of avid Texas football fans, this is the time-honored rallying gesture for the University of Texas Longhorns football team.

Export it to Italy, however, and this gesture gets twisted around like a plate of spaghetti. For millions of Italians it is the *cornuto,* and it signifies an entirely different meaning. It says "You are being cuckolded!" In more kindly terms, one person is signaling to the other that "Your spouse is being unfaithful." (See Figure 2.26.) That's a far cry from "hook 'em horns" and resulted in this actual incident.

John C. Givens Jr., an officer in U.S. Army Intelligence stationed in Italy, reported that American soldiers from Texas were in a nightclub one evening when they discovered that several other GIs present were also from the state of Texas. They started signaling the Texas "hook 'em horns" gesture between them. But Italian waiters and other locals misunderstood and took immedi-

**FIGURE 2.26 In Italy, the "innocent abroad,"
a Texas football fan . . . gets sidelined!**

ate offense. What started as a friendly reunion ended up as a
room-clearing brawl.

There are different theories about how and why "horns" have
become associated with the insult of cuckoldry. One of them is that they
taunt impotence and stupidity.

But, once again, here is an example of the *yin/yang* in gestures. Where
it may signal deception and stupidity in Italy, in Brazil and Venezuela
making horns with the fingers is a sign for good luck! You can actually
buy talismans in this shape for necklaces and charm bracelets.

There are other variations as well. When these same two fingers are
pointed *at* someone, it can signify that either "the evil eye" or a "curse" is
being placed on someone. This is the case in some African countries,
where this gesture directs or places a curse. (See Figure 2.27.)

In Italy, replicas of hands showing the "horns" can be found in shop
windows as a means of warding off evil spirits. The same is true in Malta,
where fishing boats may be seen with the hands in the "horn" position
painted on them in the hope of avoiding evil mishaps.

For still another interpretation, consider this. When I was a child in
my home state of Wisconsin, my buddies and I used this very same gesture, but to us it meant neither the evil eye nor good luck. Instead we
were saying "Bull!—" or, putting it more literally, "You're full of horse
manure."

In American baseball, when a player holds up his hand with these
two fingers upright he is signaling to his teammates that "There are two
outs. Only one more to end this inning. In American football, this is the
signal for "second down."

FIGURE 2.27 An African curse.

Among three other widely separated cultures, it is considered a sign for cattle. Hindu dancers employ it to represent a bovine. A Native American might do the same, or place his fingers on his temples, pointing them inward, to represent bison. And an Australian Aborigine would do almost the same gesture as sign language for the term *cattle*.

An entirely different meaning is given to this signal among big-city street gangs in America. Members use it as a recognition sign and, among that coterie, it signifies the horns of the Devil.

There we have it: one single hand gesture—a handful of different meanings. Depending on where it is used, it can mean a college rallying sign, a signal of infidelity, a voodoolike curse, a symbol for good luck, the Devil, or "You're full of horse apples."

Finally, in Milwaukee, Wisconsin, home of numerous foundries and metal-punching factories, coarse barroom humor gives it still a different meaning. "In our taverns," Milwaukeeans explain, "when you see someone hold his hand up like that with only the two outward fingers standing upright, it simply means that a veteran, long-suffering punch press operator is ordering four beers."

3

Special Types
of Gestures

In addition to the gestures we use for day-to-day communication, there are also other forms of body language that are highly developed and used for very specific purposes. In this chapter, we'll discuss four of these special body-language systems:

- American Sign Language

- *Tai chi*

- Flirting

- Kissing

We'll also present you with a challenge: to design new gestures for some vitally important communications.

AMERICAN SIGN LANGUAGE (ASL)

The third most popular language in America—after English and Spanish—is American Sign Language (ASL). It is a visual-gestural language composed of a collection of coded gestures based on a system developed in France in the eighteenth century. It was brought to the United States by Thomas Hopkins Gallaudet, a young Congregational minister from Connecticut. After traveling to France and learning about this system of signing, Gallaudet returned to the United States, bringing a young French deaf-signing teacher, Laurent Clerc, with him. Together they developed sign language system that blended French signs with American signs. As a legacy, today deaf people in both France and the United States can recognize similarities in the signs they use.

Gallaudet's son, Edward, became the principal of the Columbia Institution for the Deaf and Dumb in Washington, D.C., which eventually became Gallaudet University, well known throughout the United States for its education of deaf and hard-of-hearing people. Incidentally, "hearing-impaired" is a widely used euphemism, but that term can be confusing because it includes aging people who are losing their hearing and whose needs are completely different from a deaf person.

Two questions often asked are these:

- Can deaf people from different countries understand each other's sign language?

Answer: No, each national language (English, German, French, etc.) has its own form of sign language. However, when deaf people from different parts of the world try to communicate, they may resort to using basic, "raw" gestures to get messages across. As a result, deaf people from different countries can communicate somewhat more easily than hearing people who do not know the local language. The World Federation of the Deaf (similar to the United Nations) has developed a list of common gestures that signing foreigners can often understand for this basic communication. It is called *Gestuno* and is not a language in itself.

- When deaf people from different nationalities try to communicate with one another, can signs be misinterpreted?

    Answer: Yes. For example, among the deaf in the United States, the upraised middle finger is rude and insulting, just as it is for hearing people. But the same sign in Thailand means "a brother," in Korea "a mountain," and in England "a holiday."

American Sign Language communicates in two forms: (1) by signing individual letters of the alphabet to spell out a word, and (2) by using other gestures that represent full individual words. For example, to ask "What is your name?" you would make the following four gestures:

what

is

your

name

To answer by spelling out your name, the signs would be:

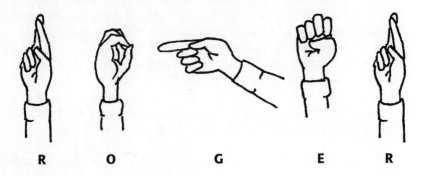

R   O   G   E   R

TAI CHI

Travel to China and you'll very likely encounter one of the oldest, most unusual series of gestural movements in the world. It is known as *tai chi* (pronounced *tie CHEE*), which is a form of exercise, a philosophy of movement, and a form of meditation all in one.

In 1967, on my first visit to Hong Kong, I arose early one morning and glanced out the window of my hotel room. There, in the park adjacent to my hotel, I saw rows and rows of Chinese men and women silently performing a type of slow-motion ballet. In almost perfect unison, each person pushed one hand forward while the other hand moved backward; each then bent one leg while extending the other; each body turned slowly in one direction, then the other—all without a single spoken command or strain of music.

What I was observing was a typical daily session of *tai chi* and, over the years, I would see this scene repeated in the hills of Taiwan, the courtyards of Beijing, and, more recently, in exercise rooms of my health club in the United States.

According to Danny Conner, author of the book *Tai Chi* (Stanley Paul & Co. Ltd., London, 1989), legend says *tai chi* was first developed in China during the Sung dynasty (A.D. 960–1279). In the late eighteenth century it became a method of boxing known as *tai chi chuan*. Since then, many of the more violent movements (foot-stamping, leaps, and explosive techniques) have been replaced by the current more relaxed and graceful form of meditative exercise.

After many years of study and practice, *tai chi* users claim multiple benefits ranging from improved physical and mental health to the mystical ability of being able to resist physical attack with a few simple, nonviolent gestures.

As for enhancing health, *tai chi* uses relaxation plus deep concentration. It requires repeated slow movement of fingers, hands, wrists, elbows, arms, waist, feet, and eyes. A complete sequence of these practiced movements can last up to thirty minutes, and adherents claim improved respiration and flexibility plus a refreshed and heightened state of mind. Some claim the concentration and movements can produce the same type of perspiration and muscle fatigue one would experience after a complete aerobic rou-

tine. *Tai chi* is said to be especially beneficial among the elderly, who claim they retain suppleness, balance, and flexibility.

If the world of acquired gestures interests you, *tai chi* is one of the oldest and most intriguing collections. On your next trip to the Far East, inquire when and where you might observe this exercise. Or, inquire at your local health club to learn if *tai chi* classes are offered. Books on *tai chi* may also be available at your local library or bookstore, but the beauty and movement are difficult to appreciate from static photos and words.

FLIRTING

Monica Moore is a psychology professor at Webster University in St. Louis who has been studying flirting for almost twenty years. She claims that American women may use fifty-two separate gestures to signal their interest in men. The most common and popular indicators are to smile, to glance, to primp, to laugh, to giggle, to toss the head, to flip hair, and to whisper. More overt movements would be hiking skirts, patting a buttock, hugging, requesting a dance, casually touching a knee or forearm, and, of course, a caress.

Moore says men don't have such a wide repertoire of motions. They may smooth their ties, brush their hands through their hair, and puff up their chests. They also smile warmly, use direct eye contact, and stand in close proximity.

Other American therapists and writers advise would-be flirters to use the following signals: say "hello" with energy; shake hands and perhaps finish the handshake with a small, extra squeeze; keep your voice soft; touch, but don't cling. Touching is a particularly strong signal, whether it is merely a gentle touch to a forearm during conversation or a swift, casual, shoulder-to-shoulder contact.

As for the rest of the world, there are two important, basic rules regarding flirtation:

1. *Be very careful*—some cultures frown on overt silent (or vocal) overtures between sexes;

2. *Be observant*—always be on the alert for gestures or signals that are new or unfamiliar to you. (See pages 85–87 for six different ways that men around the world signal the message "Oh! I see a pretty girl!")

Males from certain nationalities are known for their proclivity to signal romantic inclinations—the French, Italians, and Brazilians rank high on that list—while men from other more reserved cultures—British, Japanese, Chinese—would rarely make a flirtatious move in public. As with all such generalizations, there are exceptions among the nationalities listed here.

In a survey of American international businesswomen for the book *Do's and Taboos around the World for Women in Business* (Wiley, 1997), the following advice was offered to American women traveling abroad:

- Avoid mixing business and sex. When conducting business overseas, don't flirt under any circumstances. As one woman said: "Don't wash your feet in your drinking water."

- Be on the alert for come-ons and advances. Quash them quickly; you'll recognize them because they are usually similar all over the world.

- Avoid situations that encourage flirtation. Examples: dining alone with a new male acquaintance; offers to escort you to your hotel room; and late-night disco sessions separate from your other associates.

- Don't be insulted if men make passes at you. In many countries, it is considered a compliment. But, as mentioned earlier, quash them quickly to avoid entanglements.

KISSING

One of the few truly universal gestures is the lip kiss. Anthropologists are unsure exactly how and why the kissing gesture originated. Desmond Morris calls it a "relic gesture" passed down to us from the time when mothers would pass food, mouth-to-mouth, to their infants. Today, the act of kissing another person on the lips is common around the world. It may not be as noticeable in some cultures because of the belief that such an intimate demonstration should not occur in public.

Here are some examples of how extensively kissing has permeated our lives:

- Mothers kiss their children's bruises to "make them better."

- Tennis and golf stars kiss their newly won trophies.

- In the Gulf War of 1991, Iraqi POWs kissed the hands of their Allied Coalition captors to show their humbled state.

- In American professional basketball, at the beginning of a nationally televised championship playoff game, opponents Ervin "Magic" Johnson and Isaiah Thomas startled the sports world by kissing each other's cheek.

- We speak figuratively of "the kiss of death," whereas the act of mouth-to-mouth resuscitation is called "the kiss of life."

- In many Eastern European countries, good male friends greet each other with kisses to the cheek, often as many as three times, alternating cheeks. The number of kisses, three, is thought to be related to the Trinity.

- The French seem to revere the kiss. Xavier Fauche and Christiane Noetzin have written a 294-page book titled, simply, *Le Baiser (The Kiss)*. And in 1886 the French sculptor Auguste Rodin created one of the world's most famous sculptures, *The Kiss*.

- Hollywood, of course, has made the kiss a *geste suprême*, with Cary Grant and Ingrid Bergman holding the record for the longest and most passionate kiss ever in the film *Notorious*. Henry Fonda and Katharine Hepburn popularized a whole new term for kissing in their film *On Golden Pond* when they referred to kissing as "suck face."

- In 1996, in Lexington, North Carolina, a six-year-old boy kissed a girl classmate on the cheek at their school and created a furor that attracted media from as far away as Ireland and Australia. The reason for the uproar was that for his action, officials at the school suspended the young boy from school, sent him home, and did not allow him to go to an ice-cream party for pupils with perfect attendance. First they called the boy's action "sexual harassment" and then issued a statement saying he had broken a rule prohibiting "unwarranted and unwelcome touching of one student by another." The result was that a six-year-old's peck on the cheek could be called "the kiss heard 'round the world."

- A Gallup survey in 1992 showed that in the United States 8 percent of kissers kept their eyes open, but more than 20 percent confessed to an occasional peek. Forty-one percent said they experienced their first serious smooch when they were age thirteen, fourteen, or fifteen; 36 percent between the ages of sixteen and twenty-one. And the most memorable kiss in a motion picture was in *Gone with the Wind*, named by 25 percent.

- Author Norine Dresser tells the story of an American female author who wrote a book about the best places to kiss in and around New York City. On Valentine's Day, the author was invited aboard a cruise ship where her book was being distributed to all passengers. Americans and Europeans were delighted to meet the author and have her autograph their books. However, Japanese passengers ignored her because most Japanese disapprove of public expressions of affection; the younger generation in Japan is, however, now rebelling against this conservatism.

Finally, "deep kissing," or "deep-tongue kissing," is passionate, open-mouth kissing where the tongue explores the other person's mouth. Morris writes that it derives from the time when primitive women weaned their babies by passing chewed-up food mouth-to-mouth. It is also referred to as the "French kiss." (Author's note: As teenagers in the 1940s, it was taboo among my circle of friends to even *say* "French kiss" aloud in public. How times have changed. In 1995, Hollywood made a motion picture with that forbidden term as its title.)

In the nineteenth century, the French had a kissing game called *maraîchinage* that involved deep-tongue kissing between at least ten or more couples who changed partners weekly. In some parts of France, this "tongue dueling" was conducted in parks and even in churches. It was banned by the clergy in 1864.

For more on the act of kissing, see pages 76–79.

A CHALLENGE TO READERS

With the hundreds of gestures documented in this book, plus the thousands of other types of gestures (subconscious, instinctive, and coded), one could easily conclude that there is no room for the addition of new gestures.

Not true. And here is your opportunity to contribute to more effective social communication in the United States, Canada, and perhaps elsewhere.

Consider this setting:

You are driving on a city street, country road, or highway, and the auto in front of you has its turn signal blinking. However, the other driver continues straight ahead, neither changing lanes nor turning. You conclude, correctly, that the other driver has merely forgotten to turn off the indicator.

Challenge: How can we politely signal to another driver about this momentary forgetfulness?

As mentioned later in this book, in South Africa they have adopted a gesture for precisely this situation. It is called the "hand flap" (see page 99), which involves flapping the fingers down against the thumb.

It's possible that in America this gesture might be construed as representing the mouth, thus signaling "Talk, talk, talk." Still, if done while passing another auto, the South African version might be useful on U.S. and Canadian highways and perhaps elsewhere around the world. Do you have a better suggestion?

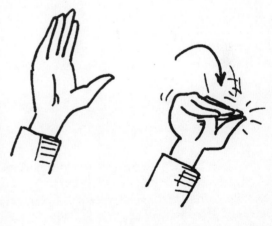

Let's continue. Here's another challenge involving driver politeness:

Let's say you inadvertently cut in front of another driver; or you pull out into traffic a bit hastily causing an oncoming car to brake; or you commit any other such minor driving offense.

Challenge: How might we gesture a friendly message that signifies "Oh! I'm sorry. I realize I made a mistake. Excuse me."

In America, we haven't yet discovered any commonly understood signal for this situation. We might throw up our hands, tilt our head, or grimace. But that could easily be misinterpreted as anger or frustration rather than as an apology. So, how should we signal the message "Ooops! I'm sorry"?

If you have recommendations for resolving these two puzzles, send them to the author, via the publisher, at the following address:

Roger Axtell
c/o John Wiley & Sons, Publishers
605 Third Avenue
New York, NY 10158–0012

Your ideas, with full accreditation, will be forwarded to the American Automobile Association and the National Safety Council.

4

Gestures:
Head to Toe

This chapter presents a *catalog of gestures* arranged by body part, starting at the head and moving down the length of the body, as follows:

Head and Face	Chin
Eyes	Arms
Ears	Hands
Nose	Fingers
Cheeks	Legs and Feet
Lips and Mouth	Full Body

If you are curious about a particular gesture you have observed, first determine which part of the body plays the most important role. Is it the head? The hands? Then turn to that section in this chapter and scan the headings and illustrations for the gesture you had in mind. You will find some duplications where gestures involve more than one part of the body.

HEAD AND FACE

The head and face are the most expressive and impressive parts of the body. Our faces are capable of showing anger, pain, joy, shock, sorrow, confidence, exhaustion, surprise, suspicion, bewilderment, boredom, cunning, doubt, and more. The face can pout, grimace, snarl, wince, blush, blanch, gape, smirk, glare, or frown. The head can nod, shake, jerk, tilt, bob, waggle, thrust, duck, turn, and even shiver.

We send scores of messages each day using just the head and face. Pantomimists learn them all. The late comedian, movie star, and story-teller Danny Kaye traveled the world enchanting audiences of children with his stories, while never knowing or speaking one word of their language.

And then there is the smile. A Wayne State University researcher claims that there are some 1,814,400 different kinds of smiles. While that may seem far-fetched, consider that just one of those smiles has been mystifying art lovers for centuries: the Mona Lisa smile. The true meaning behind her smile remains an enigma. (For more on smiles, see p. 117.)

The head and face are wonderfully versatile instruments for communications. Here are some examples.

FIGURE 4.1 Nodding and shaking the head mean different things to different people.

As we all know, *nodding the head* up and down signals "yes," and shaking it back and forth means "no." Elementary. We all send messages this way every day (Figure 4.1). But consider these contradictions:

In Bulgaria, parts of Greece, the former Yugoslavia, Turkey, Iran, and Bengal it is *the reverse*. There, among the older generation, nodding the head up and down means "no." And shaking the head back and forth means "yes." (If you've got that, now shake your head back and forth—"yes.")

Another variation occurs in Greece. There, tipping the head back rather abruptly (or, jerking the chin up) while raising the eyebrows means "no." To indicate "yes" in Greece, drop the chin down several times.

Still another variation involves the nod backward accompanied by a clicking of the tongue. In Saudi Arabia, Greece, Bulgaria, and some other parts of the Middle East, this means "no."

In Greece, tilting the whole head from side-to-side laterally means "no."

Confused? So were the Russians who occupied Bulgaria in the nineteenth century. Respecting local customs, Russian soldiers tried to discipline themselves to nod up and down when they meant "no" and to shake their heads when they wanted to signal "yes." The problem was that the Bulgarians never knew if the Russians were "speaking" in Bulgarian or their own language, so the use of head signals for communications broke down.

Charles Darwin theorized that both movements mimic infantile nursing patterns: The forward head nod is seen as part of the breast-seeking or breast-accepting pattern, and the head-shaking gesture is a sign of refusal.

The *tossing the head* backward negation gesture of Greece is also used in southern Italy, Malta, and Tunisia (Figure 4.2). But in Germany and

FIGURE 4.2   Tossing the head backward.

Scandinavia it becomes a beckoning motion. And in India, it means "yes." With remote groups like the Maoris in New Zealand, the Tagals of the Philippines, and the Dyaks of Borneo, it means "yes" as in "Yes, of course."

Tapping the head with the forefinger has a variety of meanings, some of them opposites (Figure 4.3). In Argentina and Peru it can mean "I'm thinking." If the tapping is done near the temple, it can mean "That's very intelligent." Yet in North America and other places, it can either mean "that person is very intelligent," or "that person is tetched, crazy." It all depends on the statement accompanying the gestures. In Holland, if the finger is tapped to the *center of the forehead*, it means "He's crazy."

**FIGURE 4.3   The meaning of a tap
on the head can depend on where you tap.**

Covering the head is a requirement for Jewish men and women in conservative or orthodox synagogues, for women entering certain Catholic religious shrines, and for Muslim women in public places at all times. According to the protocol of Catholicism, when women meet the Pope they must wear a shawl or other covering on their heads.

Slapping the hand to the back of the head is, according to author and anthropologist David Givens, an automatic gesture done by most cultures and designates being disturbed or startled. Other anthropologists report some Bolivian Indian tribes indicate both anger and joy by slapping the back of the head.

Rocking the head slowly, back and forth, side-to-side, is a gesture used in India and means "Yes, I am listening." At first observation, Westerners confuse this as meaning "no."

Scratching the head is a gesture occurring all over the world and thought to be almost instinctive. It signals "I am confused" or "I am skeptical."

(There are many gestures involving the head in conjunction with the hands or fingers. Where these are predominantly motions involving the hands or fingers, they will be found later in this chapter under the sections devoted to that part of the body.)

EYES

"Look me in the eye, son" is a command that's been repeated countless times through the centuries in every corner of the map. But, as we will quickly learn here, some cultures are much more eye-oriented than others.

American, Canadian, British, Eastern European, and Jewish cultures favor "face-to-face" relationships. Hispanic women may often hold eye contact longer than others, even with strange men. But many Asians, Puerto Ricans, West Indians, and African Americans tend to avoid such direct eye contact.

In one region of Africa, a U.S. Peace Corps volunteer upset tribal elders because of her teaching practices. The woman required her students to look her in the eye. In that particular culture, it was not permissible for a child to look an adult in the eye. Much the same is true among Native Americans. It is impolite to look a senior person straight in the eyes; respect is shown by avoiding the eyes.

In Japan, Korea, and Thailand, it is considered rude to stare. Prolonged direct eye contact is considered impolite and even intimidating. A few shrewd Japanese negotiators have learned that Westerners expect averted eyes, so at the bargaining tables the Japanese do *just the opposite.* They sit and stare. This is so atypical of the Japanese that it can

FIGURE 4.4   Variations of the *eyebrow flash*.

completely unnerve Westerners and cause them to disclose their next compromise.

In Saudi Arabia, one is expected to maintain strong eye contact because of the adage "The eyes are the windows to the soul." However, when doing this, visitors often become concerned by the languid, or half-shut, appearance of the eyes of many Middle Easterners, which should not be interpreted as disinterest.

The *eyebrows* can signal several different emotions. Those two lines of facial hair can indicate anger, confusion, openness, curiosity, and even flirtation (Figure 4.4).

When humans are alerted, the pupils are dilated and the eyebrows are raised. When threatened or angry, humans lower the eyebrows. In Peru, raising the eyebrows can mean "money" or "Pay me." In Tonga, it would mean "yes" or "I agree."

The *eyebrow flash* is, in America and elsewhere, a sign of flirtation used by men when they see a pretty girl. It may have been popularized by the 1930s film star Groucho Marx, noted for his heavily painted eyebrows, which he repeatedly flashed up and down while leering at pretty women.

Wetting the little finger and drawing it across the *eyebrow* is a signal sometimes used among men in the United States to indicate that some other person is homosexual. It mimics the feminine action of applying eyebrow makeup.

Blinking the eyes can also have meaning, depending on the culture. In Taiwan and Hong Kong, repeatedly blinking the eyes at someone is considered impolite.

Among Americans and Europeans, *winking* with one eyelid signifies some shared secret, yet it is regarded as impolite in Hong Kong (Figure 4.5). In the United States, it is also a rather bold, flirtatious gesture, but in Australia it is improper to wink at women.

FIGURE 4.5 The single eyelid wink.

The *eyelid pull* (pulling a corner of one eye down with the index finger) conveys "alertness," but with several related variations (Figure 4.6). For example, in places like England and France, it means "You can't fool me. I see what you're up to." But in Italy, it means "Be careful. Pay attention. Keep your eyes peeled." There, it may also hint "Be careful—he's a crook." And in the former Yugoslavia it can mean sadness or disappointment, as if a tear were falling. It might be used, for example, by one tour guide signaling to a colleague that "I got no tip from this tourist."

Rolling the eyes is a fairly common gesture around the world, and suggests incredulity or amazement.

Closed eyes do not necessarily indicate boredom or sleep. In Japan, as we learned in the incident with the governor and the American businessman visiting Japan (page 10), it may be used when a Japanese listener is in deep concentration.

FIGURE 4.6 The eyelid pull.

FIGURE 4.7 The earlobe flick.

EARS

The *earlobe flick* may be seen in Italy where touching or holding or tugging or flicking the earlobe signifies that some other person is effeminate or homosexual (Figure 4.7). It probably stems from the feminine habit of wearing earrings. In Russia it has a different meaning; it says, "I dislike that person," and it is probably meant to say, "and he should be punished, like a child."

The *ear grasp* in India is a sign of apology, as when a servant drops a dish or commits some other error (Figure 4.8).

In Brazil, *pinching the earlobe* with the thumb and forefinger is a way of expressing appreciation, as when you wish to signal you have enjoyed

FIGURE 4.8 The ear grasp.

FIGURE 4.9 Either you're crazy or you have a phone call.

a meal. Some Brazilians, to add further emphasis, will reach around over the top of the head and grasp the opposite earlobe.

Cupping the ear with one hand is understood almost universally to mean "I can't hear you."

Rotating the forefinger around in front of the ear has two entirely different meanings: in the United States, it usually connotes that someone or something is "crazy"; yet in Argentina, it can be a signal to indicate "You have a telephone call." (See Figure 4.9.)

In the United States, the customary way to signal "You have a telephone call" is *holding an imaginary telephone to the ear*. A slight amplification on this motion is to hold the hand near the ear and stiffly extend the thumb and little finger outward as if to emulate the shape of a phone receiver.

NOSE

Sticking one's nose into someone else's business is only one way to communicate with the nose. It can also be tapped, circled, thumbed, wiggled, pushed, scratched, or twisted, and each action signals a meaningful message.

The *nose tap* can be seen in England and in Italy, but the meaning is slightly different in each locale (Figure 4.10). In England it probably means confidentiality, as in "Don't spread this around," or "Let's keep this between us only." On the other hand, in Italy it is more of a friendly warning: "Watch out. Take care."

The *nose circle* may be seen in Colombia and is made by forming a circle with the thumb and forefinger and placing it over the nose (Figure 4.11). In Colombia, it signals that the person in question is homosexual.

FIGURE 4.10   The nose tap.

Making a *"V" over the nose* with the forefinger and middle finger with the palm inward toward the face is obscene in such disparate places as Saudi Arabia and Mexico (Figure 4.12). This gesture transforms the tip of the nose into a symbolic phallus.

Thumbing the nose is an almost universally known insulting gesture (Figure 4.13). It is often used by children (and others!) who want to mock one another with derision. Added emphasis comes when two hands are joined in tandem. (See the section on "Insulting Gestures" in Chapter 2 for more information.)

The *nose twist* is apparently totally unique to France. There it signifies drunkenness and may be used by one person signaling to a second person that a third party has become drunk. (See Figure 4.14.)

FIGURE 4.11   The nose circle.

FIGURE 4.12   A Saudi obscenity.

Wiggling the nose, in Puerto Rico, asks the question, "What's going on?" (In other countries it probably just means the nose-wiggler has an itch.)

Wrinkling the nose in the United States and many other countries is an indication of disgust, as expressed in the phrases "I don't like that," or "I'm disgusted." It can also pose the question, "What's that smell?"

Holding the nose with thumb and forefinger is a fairly universal and well-understood sign that means "Something smells bad." In Hollywood, it has the distinctive meaning that the product viewed is a flop.

FIGURE 4.13   Thumbing the nose.

FIGURE 4.14   Oo-la-la! A jug of wine, and thou.

Scratching or rubbing the side of the nose can, according to author and anthropologist Julius Fast, be an unconscious signal that someone is telling a lie. "Watch politicians when they speak, and if they stroke the side of their nose with their forefinger it usually means I'm going to say something outrageous . . . or I'm telling a barefaced lie."

Finally, two unique gestures involving the nose are shown here:

In Japan, when a person speaks about himself, he will often point to his nose, whereas in the West, a person usually motions toward his chest.

And in France, pushing one's nose upward with the first two fingers is a way of saying, "Oh, that's so easy I could do it with my fingers up my nose."

CHEEKS

This part of the body has been memorialized metaphorically in the Bible with the admonishment to "turn the other cheek." That gesture of forgiveness is urged when one is offended or injured by an adversary. On the other hand, the British call someone "cheeky" if he or she is impudent, bold, or brassy.

The *cheek screw* is primarily an Italian gesture of praise, as when observing a pretty girl. Here the extended forefinger is rotated, or turned into the cheek (Figure 4.15). It is rarely seen or understood—with this meaning—outside of Italy. In Germany, it has an entirely different message: "That's crazy."

A variation on this gesture would be to press the thumb and forefinger together and twist them into the cheek. Again, seen only in Italy, it would mean "attractive" or "good" or "pretty."

The *cheek stroke* in Greece, Italy, and Spain means "attractive" and would be one way of signaling "I see a pretty girl." In the former Yugoslavia, it signifies "success." In the United States, it can also be a sign of contemplation, as if saying, "That's interesting—let me think about that." In a scattering of other countries, it can mean "ill" or "thin." This gesture can be done with the thumb and other fingers stroking each side of the face, or with just the thumb and forefinger stroking downward on either side of the face. (See Figure 4.16.)

Cheek-kissing is not as simple as it may sound. In places like Russia, and perhaps the Middle East, they actually *kiss* the cheek. In other places—like France or Italy or throughout Latin America—it is considered "kissing the air." That means cheeks touch and the lips make the sound of kissing, but the lips don't actually press against the cheek.

FIGURE 4.15   The cheek screw.

FIGURE 4.16   The cheek stroke.

For the uninitiated, the quandary becomes "How many times does one kiss? Once? Or on both cheeks?" In the countries of Latin America in which cheek-kissing is practiced, only one cheek is usually kissed. In places like France, they may kiss twice (once on each cheek). And in Belgium and Russia, they may kiss three times—one side, then the other, and back to the first side.

But even before the one-two-three quandary comes the more basic question "How do you know when to kiss cheeks and when not to? When am I expected to buss and when not?" The answer comes from a slight tugging with the hand. As you shake hands with someone, if that other person believes she (or he) knows you well enough, you may feel a slight pulling on your hand. That's the signal to move in (go to *your* left, otherwise you'll bump noses) and press cheeks. One seasoned world traveler comments, "You'll quickly learn when a woman acquaintance expects you to kiss her cheek—she just reels you in with her hand."

LIPS AND MOUTH

Our lips and mouth send not only verbal signals but a whole collection of nonverbal communiqués. We pout, whistle, yawn, smile, bite, point, sneeze, and spit—each sending its own special unspoken message.

But the winner as the strongest lip-mouth communicator of all is the *kiss*. (See Chapter 3 for more on kissing.)

In parts of Asia, kissing is considered an intimate sexual act and not permissible in public, even as a social greeting.

Among the Tapuya of South America, kisses are exchanged *only* among the males as a sign of peace.

Making a kissing *sound* is a mul-
timeaning gesture. In Mexico, it is
used to beckon a waiter in a restaurant. In the Philippines, street vendors use this familiar sound to
attract the attention of potential customers. And in a wide variety of
places around the world, men use
the kissing sound as a crude but
obvious way of "commenting" on
the passing of a pretty woman.

Kissing the hand as a form of
greeting is regarded by most as a
Continental gesture of worldliness and gentility, although perhaps not to
the degree shown here. (See Figure 4.17.) A French book on etiquette says,
"The man should simply bow low over a woman's hand without actually touching it with his lips, unless it is more than just a polite greeting."

The *fingertip kiss* is also strongly identified with the French (who
else?). (See Figure 4.18.) It conveys several strains of the basic message
"That's good. That's great! That's beautiful!!" It can be seen in all the
Romance countries, such as France, Italy, Spain, and much of Latin
America, and can serve as a laudatory comment on anything from a bot-
tle of wine to a new Ferrari.

The origin of the fingertip kiss probably dates to the custom of
ancient Greeks and Romans who, when entering or leaving the temple,
threw a kiss to sacred objects such as statues and altars.

From kissing, we move now to other lip and mouth gestures:

Whistling in Europe, when done by crowds, is a form of jeering. But
not so in the United States, where whistling usually conveys approval.

FIGURE 4.17   More than just a polite greeting?

FIGURE 4.18   The fingertip kiss.

And in India it is downright impolite to whistle in public. Americans *hiss* and *boo* to express disapproval. Europeans hiss for silence. In places like Haiti and Spain, they will make noises like "hssssst" and "pssssst" to attract the attention of someone.

Spitting is another sometimes mixed-up signal. For most cultures, spitting in public is considered a rude, crude act. Spitting at someone is an insult, tantamount to a slap in the face.

In other places, spitting has kinder meanings. In the first century A.D., Pliny mentions it as a means of averting witchcraft. The emperor Vespasian, according to Tacitus, cured a blind man by placing his spit on the man's eyes. Both Mark and John also claim in the New Testament that spit applied to the eyes of a blind man restored his sight, adding even further weight to the power of human saliva.

In the People's Republic of China, spitting in public is almost commonplace because there it is regarded as an act of hygiene. It is ridding the body of a waste. The same with blowing the nose, which may be done directly on to the ground, without benefit of a handkerchief. When I once expressed distaste over this custom, my Chinese host said, "What's wrong with it? What do *you* do?" When I explained I used a handkerchief for blowing my nose, he countered with, "But then you put it back into your pocket. That means you actually carry it around with you all day, doesn't it?"

In 1975, American diplomat Cyrus Vance, soon to become U.S. Secretary of State, kept his cool when confronted by this business of spitting. He was seated next to China's leader, Deng Xiaoping, and as was the custom, between their chairs was a spittoon. Whenever Deng would clear his throat and lean over to expectorate, Vance showed no reaction whatsoever. Observers did note, however, that each time Deng spat, Vance instinctively shifted his foot six inches farther away from the spittoon, then returned it when Deng was finished.

Yawning is a universal sign of tiredness, boredom, or both. But in many countries (France, Belgium, Germany, the United States, Canada, and others) yawning in public is considered impolite . . . and especially so if one does not cover the mouth with the hand. Incidentally, professional speaker H. V. Prochnow defines "protocol" as "learning to yawn with your mouth closed."

Any display of the *open mouth* is considered very rude in Asian countries, particularly Japan and Korea. Have you ever noticed that many Asians, especially women, cover their mouths when they smile, laugh, or giggle? This is the reason.

In Japan, it is also considered impolite to show your teeth in public, or to sneeze or blow your nose at a business or social gathering.

The *lip point* is a substitute for pointing without using the hand or finger. It is common among Filipinos, Native Americans, Puerto Ricans, and many Latin Americans. The action involves pursing the lips and motioning them in the desired direction.

The *teeth flick*, or "thumbnail flick" as it was called in Chapter 2, involves placing the thumbnail under the upper teeth and then flicking the thumb and fist outward. While it was known and used in Elizabethan England, it is now primarily an Italian gesture meaning anger or a curse or the equivalent of saying, "You are nothing!" A variation may be found in the former Yugoslavia, where the teeth are used to *bite the knuckle* of the forefinger, a gesture that sends the same message.

Picking the teeth with a toothpick in public is, in Italy, a sign that the cuisine was appreciated. In Asia, it is often done at the dinner table, but always with the other hand discreetly covering the mouth.

The *tongue*, as an instrument of communication, not only helps shape our spoken words but also conveys important unspoken messages. Sticking out the tongue can (1) express derision, as when children stick out their tongues at others, (2) underscore concentration, as when we focus intently on some job at hand, (3) serve as a sexual lure, as when we slowly wet or lick our lips when attracted to another, or (4) indicate greeting, as in some parts of Tibet where people greet one another by sticking out their tongues.

CHIN

In England, the chin is also called the "the pecker," probably because it is involved in "pecking" food. Americans are startled when they hear a Britisher say "Keep your pecker up" (meaning "Keep your chin up").

FIGURE 4.19   The chin flick.   FIGURE 4.20   The chin stroke.

Whatever you call it, the chin plays just as important a role in our body language as any other part of the body. Some examples follow.

The *chin flick* involves brushing the fingernails of one hand under the chin and then continuing in an outward motion, away from the chin (Figure 4.19). As with many gestures, this one has variable meanings, depending on the region:

- In France and northern Italy, it means "Get lost. You are annoying me."

- In southern Italy, it is negative but not insulting. It could mean "There is nothing," or "no," or "I cannot."

- In Tunisia, it is insulting.

- In France, it symbolizes a man's beard. Therefore, as an insult it is saying, "I throw my masculinity at you."

The *chin stroke* is also associated with a real or imaginary beard, and is therefore a masculine gesture (Figure 4.20). It suggests either (1) contemplation, as if saying "I am thinking," or (2) admiration, as when a man admires a fine painting, a fine car, or a beautiful woman.

The *chin toss* is the same gesture as the *head toss*. The head jerks back and the chin moves upward. It is used as a negation in southern Italy, Malta, Greece, and Tunisia. In Germany and Scandinavia, it is a beckoning motion. In India, it means "yes."

If you *stroke an imaginary beard under your chin*, in several central European countries you are sending any one of several messages: "I am bored," "This is taking too long," or "That story is so old (or so long) I could grow a beard." You may observe this gesture in countries such as France, Italy, Holland, and Germany.

Finally, why do we clasp our hands under our chins when we pray? It comes from the Middle Ages, when sign language was the chief means of communicating in monasteries and nunneries. The monks and nuns would clasp their hands under their chins to avoid interruption while praying, and this devotional pose has continued through the centuries.

ARMS

A soccer player, after scoring a goal, thrusts his arms upward and races toward his teammates filled with joy and pride. A boxer, after knocking an opponent senseless, stands over the body, arms raised in obvious glory and triumph. Yet, at the opposite pole is the picture of a defeated soldier raising his arms into the air in surrender, in this case signaling "I carry no weapon."

Curiously, the dramatic gesture of *upraised arms* can signal directly opposite meanings: victory or surrender (Figure 4.21).

FIGURE 4.21　Victory or surrender.

**FIGURE 4.22   There are actually six
different ways we fold our arms.**

Furthermore, politicians raise the arms to incite a crowd, religious followers use them to praise a divine spirit, and an audience of deaf people
signal both praise and applause by raising their arms and wiggling their
palms.

Sports officials in almost every sporting game have a maze of arm signals to communicate decisions to spectators. The system for signaling
with arms and flags, called "semaphore," has been used for centuries
aboard ships and on railroad lines.

Some cultures, like the Italians, use the arms freely and enthusiastically. Others, like the Japanese, are more reserved; it is considered impolite in Japanese social or business situations to gesticulate with broad
movements of the arms.

Folded arms are interpreted by some social observers as a form of body
language that says, "I am taking a defensive posture," or "I disagree with
what I am hearing." True or not, anthropologists explain that there are
actually *six* different ways we fold our arms—and we each have our own
favorite way (Figure 4.22). Try it as an experiment. Take your customary
position; then enfold your arms in a different form; for most it will feel
slightly uncomfortable.

Arms akimbo involves standing with the hands on the hips, elbows
bowed outward (Figure 4.23). In many cultures, this stance signals
aggression, resistance, impatience, or even anger. In fact, the word *akimbo*
comes from the Old Norse, meaning "bent like a bow," as if to suggest an
archer's bow that is bent to launch an arrow.

Tapping the elbow of one arm with the other hand (Figure 4.24) is, in
Colombia and a few other Latin areas, a way of saying "He's cheap" or
"stingy." In the Netherlands, it could mean "He's unreliable." A variation
on this is found in Mexico, where if you lift your left forearm vertically

FIGURE 4.23 Arms akimbo.

and hit the bottom of the elbow with the palm of the other hand, as if swatting a mosquito, it is considered an insult.

Arms behind the back, hands grasped is, according to some psychologists, a sign of ease and control. It is a way of saying, "I am exposing the front of my body. I have nothing to fear."

The *arm brush* (Figure 4.25) is seen in the Arab cultures and is a way of saying "No way! You are exaggerating." It is done by waving the hand back and forth across the front of the body below the waist.

An almost universal idiosyncrasy involving the arms occurs when we give directions. If the destination is close, our elbow is bent and the finger is about shoulder high; however, if the destination is far away, we lift the arm higher and stretch it out almost full length. Incidentally, in Japan and China it is more polite when pointing to use the full hand rather than

FIGURE 4.24 Tapping the elbow means "He's cheap."

FIGURE 4.25   The arm brush.

the index finger. Malaysians use the thumb to point, while Native Americans use the chin or "lip pout" rather than pointing with the hand or finger.

Probably the most famous arm gesture of all, though, is the *forearm jerk*, which uses the forearm and hand as an exaggerated phallic symbol (Figure 4.26). No matter the country or language, it is a strong insulting gesture. If you are on the receiving end, beware, be cautious.

FIGURE 4.26   The most famous arm gesture.

HANDS

Here's a quick test. Ask someone to describe a spiral staircase. Or, ask them to describe an accordion. Nine out of ten people will use their hands, first in a spiral to show how the staircase winds up or down, and then squeezing back and forth across the chest, as when playing an accordion. It's almost automatic, irresistible.

Of all the body parts, the hands are probably used most for sending nonverbal signals. Can there be a more impressive depiction of the hand as a powerful communicator than Michelangelo's painting of the Creator reaching out to touch man's hand?

Desmond Morris observes that we use the hands like a baton to emphasize the rhythm and intent of our words. Furthermore, he proposes that the Italians are the best baton wielders, while the Japanese are the least enthusiastic baton signalers.

Let's look at the baton signals used when a macho male wants to signal the ubiquitous message "Oh! What a pretty girl!" If you had a mixed group of men—say an Italian, a Greek, a Brazilian, a Frenchman, and an Arab—you'd see more than a half-dozen different versions of expressing that same thought. Here's how men in those different countries might signal with the hands that they *see a pretty girl*.

- An Italian may use the *cheek screw* as if he were creating a dimple.

- A Greek *strokes his cheek* because in ancient times an egg-shaped face was considered especially beautiful.

- A Brazilian forms two tubes with his hands as though he is *looking through a telescope.*

- A Frenchman *kisses his fingers,* which has become known as a special Gallic gesture of praise, whether it be for a pretty woman or a memorable wine.

- An Arab may *stroke his beard.*

 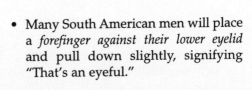

- Many South American men will place a *forefinger against their lower eyelid* and pull down slightly, signifying "That's an eyeful."

- An old Italian gesture seen in old American silent movies was the *moustache twist,* which suggests a man must preen himself in preparation for his advances toward a girl.

- And finally, in many cultures a man will use both hands to *sweep down an imaginary feminine body* to signal "What a shape!"

Hand-clapping, or applause, is an almost universal way for audiences to express praise and appreciation. But even that common action has its variations:

- Russians and Chinese groups may use applause to *greet* someone. Also, at the conclusion of a performance, ballet performers in Russia will often applaud back to an appreciative audience, an act that some Westerners misinterpret as egotism.

- Right-handers pound their favored hand down on to the palm of the left hand when applauding; left-handers do the opposite.

- In almost all countries, when seated audiences wish to pay special tribute, say, to a head of state or for a superlative performance, they will rise and give a *standing* round of applause.

- In many European countries, particularly in central and eastern Europe, audiences frequently *clap in rhythm* as a sign of approval. This is most frequently done at ice skating exhibitions, perhaps because the audience is also keeping time with the musical accompaniment. Visitors to North America, however, should know that slow, rhythmic clapping signals *impatience.*

- When the Milwaukee Symphony Orchestra toured Japan, they learned about Japanese concert customs. For example, Japanese audiences applaud until the players leave the stage. (Orchestras in the United States don't leave until the audience stops clapping.) And when Japanese audiences wave at the performers, it is considered a great compliment. But when the members of the Milwaukee group learned this, they waved back . . . which just started the Japanese clapping again.

Handshaking, as a greeting, is discussed in full detail beginning on page 17.

Hand-holding among males is a custom of special friendship and respect in several Middle Eastern countries. It can also be seen in places

like Korea, parts of China, and Indochina. In those parts of the world, it should not be misconstrued as an indication of homosexuality. In parts of North America, however, particularly in cities with large gay populations like San Francisco or New York, it is common to see two gay men proudly exhibiting their affection via this gesture.

The *right hand* has special significance in many societies. For example, in courtrooms, witnesses are asked to raise their right hand to swear oaths of truthfulness. Also, the idiom "a left-handed compliment" means an insincere or twisted compliment, and the French word for left, *gauche,* in English means "crude" or "awkward." As a result, in certain countries in the Middle East and in Asia, it is best to present business cards or gifts, or to pass dishes of food, using only the right hand.

The *left hand* is considered the "unclean" hand in much of the Middle East because it is customarily reserved for bodily hygiene. There, lavatories are often not equipped with either a toilet bowl or toilet tissue. Bathrooms frequently consist of just a hole in the floor, perhaps with indentations on either side for the feet, plus a nearby water faucet. There may also be a small pitcher in which to pour the water on to the hands. Thus, one cleans oneself with the left hand and the water.

This custom is especially important to remember because, as a consequence, at communal dinners where food is often touched with the hands, the left hand should *never* be used for eating. Furthermore, as a form of punishment in that part of the world, criminals have their right hands amputated. That person is forced to live with only one hand, the "unclean" hand, and will probably be shunned by society as a result.

Hand waves, used for greetings or beckoning or farewells, are described in detail in Chapter 2, beginning on page 25. There you will find more information on the following common hand gestures used for greeting or beckoning another person:

- The *namaste,* or *wai,* where the hands are in a praying position, is the customary greeting in places like India and Thailand.

- The *salaam*, a sweeping motion with the hand, going from heart to head and outward, is still used in parts of the Middle East.

As for waving "hello" or "good-bye," or when trying to gain someone's attention, there are actually *three different* signals:

- The *hand waggle*, with the whole hand waggling back and forth, left to right, is the custom in North America.

- The *hand bob*, with the hand bobbing up and down at the wrist, as if patting some object, is more common in Europe.

- The *palm upward, finger-scratching* inward motion is peculiar to Italy.

When *beckoning* someone in the United States, the hand may be raised and the *index finger curled* back and forth. However, in places like Japan, Indonesia, Hong Kong, Australia, and others, this is used only for calling animals, so it would be impolite to direct at any human.

The *hand push* is peculiar to Greece and is considered an insulting gesture. It originates from ancient times when dirt or even feces were rubbed in the face of captured enemies.

More *insulting hand gestures* are illustrated and described in Chapter 2 (see pages 30–39). Here is a brief review of the main ones:

- *The finger* is usually accompanied by a jerking upward motion of the hand. It is a phallic symbol and says, "Up yours!"

- The *ear waggle* uses the hands at either side of the head to imitate a donkey, which is considered slow and stupid.

- *Thumbing the nose* involves the thumb and hand extending from the nose and is an age-old mocking gesture used by many cultures.

- The *thumbnail flick* or *thumb bite* is performed by making a fist with the hand and pretending to bite the tip of the thumb or thumbnail. It is synonymous with the word *insult*.

- *Shaking the fist* is an almost universal gesture signaling anger, resentment, and opposition.

- *Slapping a fist* upward into the palm of the other hand is, in such widely separated places as France and Chile, a demonstrative way of saying "Up yours!"

FIGURE 4.27   A sexual insult.

Another insulting gesture among males (also considered vulgar) is the *crotch grab*. As the name implies, it simply involves grabbing the genitals with one hand, usually rather vigorously. The meaning is strongly sexual and insulting. In Argentina, the same message is sent by a man who uses both hands to slap down and grab his own inner thighs.

A related sexual insult seen in parts of South America is the *cupping of the hands* (Figure 4.27). This is done in the following manner: A man holds his hands in the shape of two cups slightly below the waist and makes an up-and-down motion, as if holding two heavy weights. The implication is that these are heavy testicles, thus sending the message that the other person is incapable of having successful sex with a woman.

The *hand purse* is as Italian as pizza, pasta, and the Tower of Pisa (Figure 4.28). Among Italians, it is used for punctuating and emphasizing speech. It also conveys different emotions. For example, if the fingers are gripped tightly and the hand jerked abruptly, it conveys strength or anger. If the fingers are gripped lightly and the motion is gentle, it might signal precision or delicacy. Indeed, there are so many nuances to this distinctly Italian gesture that it could warrant a special guidebook of its own. Incidentally, it may be seen in a few other European countries, but Italy is truly its home territory.

FIGURE 4.28   The hand purse.

The *fig* is one of the more confusing hand gestures because in some countries it is an insult, in others it sends sexual signals, and in still other parts of the world it is a signal for "good luck." (See Figure 4.29.)

Desmond Morris claims that the *fig*—a clenched fist with the thumb coming through between the knuckle of the index and middle fingers—was popular in ancient Rome where it represented a "penis inserted through labia." Through the ages, this was somehow twisted around to also convey good luck. Here are three regions where these separate interpretations prevail:

- In Brazil, replicas of this gesture have become a popular charm for necklaces or bracelets because it is believed this gesture wards off evil. There it is called the *figa*, incidentally, and means "good luck."

- In Greece and Turkey, it is considered an insulting gesture, as if displaying the symbolic phallus in a taunting fashion.

- In Tunisia and Holland, it has strong sexual connotations.

As if to add even further confusion, it has yet a fourth meaning in the former Yugoslavia. There it is used to signal "nothing," as when a mother might say to a child, "No, you cannot have any ice cream."

FIGURE 4.29   The fig.

FIGURE 4.30   "Hang loose."

As for historical documentation for this gesture, Dante, in his *Inferno* (*XXV*, 1–3) wrote: "When he had finished, the thief—to his disgrace— raised his arms with both fists making figs, and cried, 'Here God. I throw them in your face!' "

The *hang loose* gesture with thumb and little finger extended is popular in Hawaii and is a way of saying "Stay cool," or "Relax." (See Figure 4.30.) In Mexico, when this gesture is done vertically in front of the body (knuckles pointing outward) it means "Would you like a drink?" In this case, the hand and fingers represent a handle to a mug. And in Japan, this positioning of the fingers signals the number "six," since the thumb represents "five" and the little finger adds one more digit to equal "six."

A variation on the "hang loose" gesture is the American Sign Language shorthand version of the message "*I love you.*" (See Figure 4.31.) You may see rock stars, politicians, clergy, and others flashing this signal

FIGURE 4.31   American Sign Language shorthand for "I love you."

FIGURE 4.32   The high five.

to their audiences. Also, GIs in Operation Desert Storm were seen flashing this gesture at TV cameras.

The *high five* gesture (Figure 4.32) is just one of many transitory gestures given to us by the sports world. Sports commentator Al McGuire
claims in America it's fading out, as many sports gestures do, and is now
considered a "yuppie move." Professional baseball players in the United
States now bump forearms, football players bump helmets, and basketball players bump chests. Soccer players around the world run wildly and
leap into each other's arms after scoring a goal.

Also from the sports world is the *time-out* gesture. The hands form the
letter *T,* and it is commonly seen in American football and basketball
(Figure 4.33).

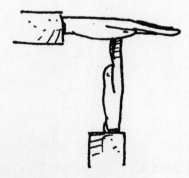

FIGURE 4.33   Time-out.

Using the *hands to measure lengths or heights* would seem a simple and uncomplicated process. But in some Latin American countries it can be a tricky business, particularly in Colombia. As for *heights*, there are two different ways, depending on if one is referring to a human or to an animal. To designate the height of an *animal*, a Colombian puts the palm downward, but to show the height of a *person*, the *edge* of the palm points downward.

Also in Colombia, one does *not* designate *lengths* by extending the forefingers of each hand as is the custom in most parts of the world. In Colombia, this is considered a rude gesture. Instead, to demonstrate the length of an object, a person extends the hand and forearm (palm held vertically) and then shows the desired length with the vertical palm of the other hand.

Suicide gestures are different, depending on the country:

- In the United States, a person points a forefinger to the temple, thumb pointing upward, to resemble a pistol.

- In Japan, a stabbing motion to the stomach conveys the same message, as if committing *hara-kiri*.

- In New Guinea, putting one hand to the throat in a choking motion is the signal for suicide.

However, in North America the choking gesture can also have two other meanings:

- In American sporting circles, it means "I choked," meaning "I tensed up" or "I froze up" and therefore performed badly.

- A far more serious interpretation is that the person is actually choking. When a person lodges a piece of food in the throat, it is impossible to cough, breathe, or talk. Bystanders often misinterpret the frantic actions of that person as a heart attack or some other malady and may apply the wrong type of first aid. As a result, the American Red Cross is trying to train people to use this choking gesture to signal "I am choking! Please help me by applying the correct aid to help dislodge food!"

Using the hand to toast others goes back to Roman times and seems a simple matter, but it can have important social nuances. For example, it is important to have good eye contact with the guest of honor or the chief host while toasting. In Asia, a toast is often accompanied by the word *Kan-pei*, which means "bottoms up," and it may even be proper protocol actually to turn your glass upside down to demonstrate that you have, indeed, emptied the glass. Also, among older, more traditional Swedes, the proper toasting motion "begins from the seventh button down on the waistcoat upward to the eyes, followed by a nod of the head, a drink, good and direct eye contact, and then lower the glass down to the seventh button once again."

Another bit of toasting lore is found in England, where even today, some pewter mugs are fitted with glass bottoms. The reason for this is that centuries ago unsuspecting sailors were shanghaied into service when a recruiter would secretly slip a coin into a mug of ale. Then, as the sailor emptied the mug, the coin would fall to his lips. At that time in England, the act of kissing the coin of the Crown was considered a form of pledging service and loyalty. As the victim drank, the coin would touch his lips, thereby unwittingly "enlisting" him into naval service. As a precaution, mugs were fitted with glass bottoms so the drinker could see what lay on the bottom and thereby avoid this unwanted gesture of fealty.

Knocking on wood can be traced back to the days before Christ. It has come to signify a jumble of meanings: showing reverence for the Christian (wooden) cross, knocking on (wooden) church doors for sanctuary, a form of tree worship, or even knocking on Heaven's door. The English say "touch wood" while Americans use "knock on wood," all to bring good luck. The Finns believe it is important to knock on bare wood, and therefore may be seen knocking *under* a table rather than on top.

The *hand pat* to the back of the hand in the Netherlands is a signal denoting that someone else is gay. It is done by brushing the fingers of one hand across or on top of the back of the other hand (Figure 4.34).

The *hand sweep* may be seen in Latin America and means that "someone is stealing" or "getting away with something." In Peru, it means

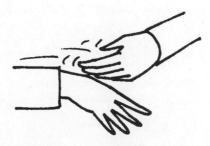

FIGURE 4.34 The hand pat.

FIGURE 4.35   The hand sweep.

"money" or "pay me." It is done by making a sweeping or grabbing motion with the hand toward the body, as though sweeping chips off a table (Figure 4.35).

The *flat hand flick* is an almost universal gesture meaning "go away" or "get lost." It is done by holding the palm downward and flicking the fingers away from the body (Figure 4.36). According to an article in the *Jerusalem Post*, to an Israeli this gesture says "Enough already," yet to an Ethiopian it means "I love you."

A *hand saw* across the forehead expresses the message "I've had it up to here," or "I'm in deep, over my head." The hand cuts across the top of the head, as if saying, "I'm in deep water up to here." (See Figure 4.37.)

The *hand wag* is performed by pointing the hand outward, palm down, fingers spread, and then waggling the whole hand up and down (thumb up, thumb down, thumb up again, and so on). (See Figure 4.38.) In the United States and Europe, it is often done in response to "How are you?" or "How does it go?" and means "Just so-so." "Not good. Not bad." In Holland and other countries, it can also be used to signal "Oh, it's very tricky."

FIGURE 4.36   The flat hand flick.

Figure 4.37 The hand saw.

The *hitchhiking* gesture is predominantly a North American gesture, used on highways to signal "I need a ride." It is done by making a fist, thumb up and then making a sweeping motion, pointing the thumb in the direction the person wishes to go. Americans should be extra cautious about exporting this gesture, however. Author James C. Simmons reports that in 1972, three young American college men were sexually assaulted while hitchhiking across Turkey from Istanbul to Ankara. In many parts of that country, he writes, this is a symbol used as an invitation for a homosexual encounter. In places like Sardinia, Greece, and parts of West Africa, it is generally an insulting gesture, meaning "Get stuffed."

The *hand flap* may be seen in South Africa. It is performed by stiffening the four fingers and flapping them down against the thumb, as if imitating the bill of a duck (Figure 4.39). I once drove from Johannesburg to

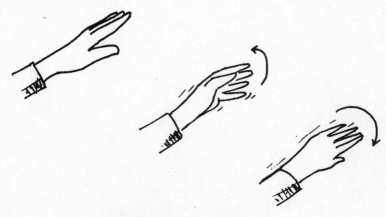

FIGURE 4.38 The hand wag.

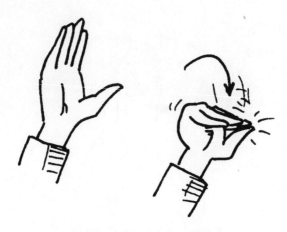

FIGURE 4.39   The hand flap.

Pretoria and spotted people along the side of the road making this gesture at me. I assumed it was some sort of greeting, so I "flapped" back at them. When I arrived in Pretoria, I got out of the car and then noticed my left turn signal had been blinking. It wasn't until that moment that I realized those helpful South Africans were signaling to me that my left turn signal was flashing on and off. And what had I done? I had signaled back to them, saying, in effect "So is yours!"

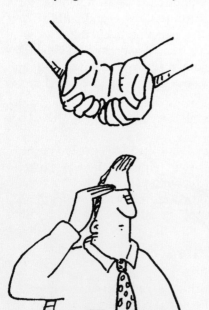

Cupped hands appear to be the universal signal for begging. In South Africa, a new arrival may observe porters at airports holding out their hands in this fashion. They are saying, "The gift you may give me for carrying your bags will mean so much, I must hold it in two hands."

Hand salute is, in many countries, the military gesture for conveying respect to a higher ranking officer. Historians believe that the salute probably originates from medieval days when knights in armor raised their visors to one another as a signal that they meant no harm. Yet, in Italy, a salute to the forehead also means "You're *pazzo* (crazy)."

FIGURE 4.40   The three-finger salute.

Before and during World War II, Adolf Hitler and his followers adopted the stiff-armed salute and now, in Germany, racist youths in their neo-Nazi fervor use a modified form: stiff arm pointing upward and outward, but with two fingers (little finger and ring finger) curled into the palm (Figure 4.40).

A similar form of this gesture is, at this writing, appearing in the streets of Belgrade, Yugoslavia. A similar *three-finger* salute, but with fingers slightly spread and arms less stiff, is being used as a rallying and unifying signal by opponents of the current Serbian president, Slobodan Milošević.

Keeping one's *hands in one's pockets* when conversing in either social or business situations is considered an impolite posture in such diverse locales as Belgium, Indonesia, France, Finland, Japan, and Sweden.

Hands on hips in Indonesia and many Latin American countries may well be interpreted as a gesture of defiance or challenge.

Some Universal Hand Gestures

- Pressing the palms together and resting the head on the back of the hand while closing the eyes as if sleeping is generally understood as saying "I am tired."

FIGURE 4.41   Are you right-thumbed or left?

- Patting the stomach with the hands usually means "I am full."

- Taking the hand and making a circular motion over the stomach signals "I am hungry."

- Using the hand to mimic the act of drinking is a way of gesturing the message "I am thirsty."

- Rubbing the hands together can mean (1) "I am cold," (2) "Oh, that's nice," (3) "It's cozy," or (4) a sign of eager anticipation.

Folded hands, with fingers intertwined, is a gesture seen around the world. But there is one peculiarity worth noting: each of us has a favorite thumb that we consistently place on top. Try it. Fold your hands in your customary fashion. Now switch the position of the thumbs. It usually feels slightly uncomfortable (Figure 4.41).

Crossing the heart with the hand is a Christian rite harking back to the crucifix. Just as many people "cross the fingers" as a pledge of faith or good luck, Christians make this sign over the upper body. According to Tad Tuleja, author of *Curious Customs* (Stonesong Press, 1987), in early times it was done with thumb and forefinger at the forehead. By the fourth century, the heart was also crossed. By the tenth century, full upper-body crossing was the custom. "From the thirteenth century on," Tuleja writes, "Eastern-rite Catholics use the thumb and first two fingers (symbolizing the Trinity) and touch the right shoulder first. Roman-rite followers use the full five digits (supposedly representing Christ's five wounds) and touch the left shoulder first."

Where do you place your hands while eating? On top of or beneath the table? American mothers teach their children to place the left hand in the lap; many European mothers teach just the opposite, that both hands should remain above or on the table. The reasons for keeping both hands visible apparently date back to the sixteenth century. One explanation is that this demonstrated that no weapons were being concealed below the table. Another is that both hands on the table assured that there was no sexual hanky-panky going on among tablemates.

FIGURE 4.42 The fist slap.

The *fist slap* in several countries (France, Italy, and Chile, to name just three) can signify a very strong, rude message saying "Up yours!" It can be done in two ways: (1) by holding the palm of one hand downward and smacking the fist of the other hand up and into that palm; (2) the fist can be held stationary and the palm of the other hand can slap down on top. Visitors to the United States should note that Americans and others may do this gesture in casual idleness, with no special significance or message. By the same token, Americans visiting the locales just noted should avoid any such casual, idle swinging and slapping of the hands (Figure 4.42).

Fist pounding is generally understood to signal anger and determination. It can be done with either hand onto a hard surface, or into the palm of the other hand. One graphic example of fist pounding was that of Soviet premier Nikita Khrushchev, who pounded first his fist and then his shoe on his desk at the United Nations back in the late 1950s.

Two fists, with thumbs tucked inside and then gently thrust in a downward motion, is a Germanic way of saying "Good luck!" (Figure 4.43.)

FIGURE 4.43 Good luck!

FIGURE 4.44   The bird flap.

While others may cross their fingers as a message and wish for good luck, Germans will use this distinctive "two fists" gesture instead.

Rapping the knuckles on wood is, according to Morris, akin to "touching the sacred oak to placate the god Thor." It is done after making a wish or boast. Swedes may rap underneath a table in order to assure touching bare wood. In Germany, however, this gesture is also used for two rather delightful welcoming messages. For example, students at universities will greet their professors at the beginning of a class by rapping knuckles on desks as a signal of greeting and respect. Also, when dining at a large communal table, as people arrive or leave the table, they may be seen and heard to rap the table lightly. It is a form of greeting or farewell and a substitute for the inconvenience of rising and walking around the table to shake hands.

The *bird flap* gesture involves placing the palm of one hand over the back of the other, with thumbs extended, and wiggling the thumbs to imitate a flying bird (Figure 4.44). In Colombia, this is a sign to denote a homosexual.

The *copulation gesture* is known in many countries and is both descriptive and graphic. The forefinger of one hand is inserted into a ring formed by the thumb and forefinger of the other hand to represent the act of copulation (Figure 4.45).

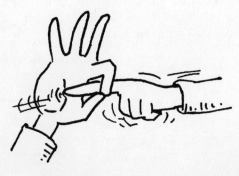

FIGURE 4.45   Nearly universal—and none too subtle.

FIGURE 4.46   How a deaf person applauds.

Now, here's a closing question. Have you ever considered how an audience of deaf people applaud? No, they don't pound their hands together to create an audible wave of sound. Rather, they have conceived a beautiful *sight* to replace the sound of applause. They raise their hands to either side of the head and waggle them furiously, creating what assuredly is a heartwarming picture of waves and waves of fingers in motion signaling this very special form of appreciation (Figure 4.46).

FINGERS

Anyone who has cut or sprained a finger knows how our lives can become instantly more cumbersome. We fumble over buttons, miss keys on computers, misdial telephones, and have trouble gripping objects. It's so vexing our whole temperament is affected. And without our fingers our daily communication would be severely warped—both our spoken and our nonverbal communication.

For example, many figures of speech rely heavily on the fingers: We speak of a finger of land; we finger cloth or a musical instrument; a snitch "fingers" a miscreant; we "wrap someone around our finger"; we burn our fingers; we put them in pies; they are indispensable for counting; our drinkers ask for "a couple fingers of whiskey"; and, finally, our fingers provide one-fifth of our senses, our sense of touch.

We use the fingers extensively in our nonverbal communication. Here are some examples.

The Finger, as we call it, is notorious worldwide. "The finger wave," the "bird," the "bone," the "one-finger salute," the "indecent finger," and the "expressway digit" are just a few of its English synonyms. Who

FIGURE 4.47   The one-finger salute.

knows how many novel synonyms exist in dozens of other languages? (See Figure 4.47.)

As we learned in Chapter 2 (see page 30), "the finger" has been used as an insult for over 2,000 years. Middle Easterners modify it by pointing it downward, and just about all historians agree it is considered rude and obscene because of its phallic symbolism.

The *"O.K." signal* was also discussed in detail in Chapter 2 (see page 43). Here, the thumb and forefinger form a simple circle . . . but then the confusion begins:

- In most societies, it is recognized as an American-born gesture for "Everything is fine," or "Everything is O.K." Desmond Morris supposes that it originates from putting the thumb and forefinger together as if holding something very small, thus suggesting "precision" or "just right."

- In France it means "zero" or "worthless," and in Japan it is the signal for money.

- And in a host of other countries—Brazil being the best known—it is considered very rude because it is seen to represent the female genitalia. Ancient vases, some 2,000 years old, depict males using this signal as an insult. And it is likely to be an insult in the following countries: Malta, Sardinia, Greece, Brazil, Tunisia, Italy, Turkey, Russia, and Paraguay.

Our *thumb* is a very special digit because of its singular versatility. It not only sets humans apart in the animal world because it affords us special grasping abilities, but it also expressively communicates so many varied messages. Here are some examples:

- We learned in Chapter 2 all about the *thumbs-up* gesture (see page 45), and how it ranges from meaning everything from "Right on!" to something very rude (in Australia, "Up yours, mate!") (Figure 4.48).

- The thumb is also the dominant feature when *hitchhiking*. But as a few Western hitchhikers have learned, in some countries (Nigeria being one), the upright thumb, whether in or not motion, is considered an insult.

- In Germany, the upright thumb is a signal for the *number* one. But in Japan, that identical upright thumb signifies the number five.

- Both the phrase and the gesture *thumbs-down* mean that something is bad or rejected, and that interpretation reaches as far back as Roman times. It is seen on ancient Roman frescoes. But, interestingly, there are no known depictions of the thumbs-up gesture as meaning "O.K." or "Good" or "He shall live," as we have been led to believe, probably by Hollywood movies.

- When Germans wish to signal "good luck," they *tuck the thumb into the fist*. They may even do it with both fists, and then make a slight up-and-down or pounding motion.

- In Malaysia, when *pointing*, the thumb is favored over the forefinger or other fingers.

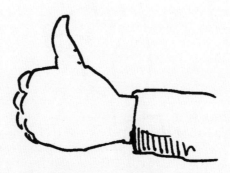

FIGURE 4.48   "Up yours, mate!"

- In Spain, displaying an upward thumb is the *symbol for support* of the Basque separatist movement, and therefore it becomes a political statement that can actually incite strong discord.

- In summary, a thumb sitting upright on a clenched fist is considered *a rude signal* in the following places: Australia (especially when jerked upward slightly), Sardinia, Greece, Turkey, Nigeria, Iran, Ghana, and Russia.

When and where the thumb is used in conjunction with the other fingers increases the message-sending possibilities manyfold. Here are some examples:

- *Rubbing the thumb and forefinger together* sends several different signals. The most common one is "money." Rubbing the thumb and forefinger back and forth in this manner apparently mimics the gesture of thumbing folding money. It also mimics the action of feeling a fabric, or accompanies the question, "What does it feel like?"

- *Squeeze the thumb and forefinger tightly together* and many people in the Mediterranean region will consider it vulgar because it supposedly depicts the vagina. Yet in France, this gesture may be used to send the visual signal that something is "perfect," as in the statement "It is *this* close . . . so close that it is almost perfect" (Figure 4.49).

Pointing with the index finger is common in North America and Europe, but it is considered impolite in Japan and China where they favor using the whole open hand. Malaysians prefer pointing with the thumb rather than the forefinger. Incidentally, among Native Americans it is con-

**FIGURE 4.49   A Mediterranean vulgarity
that is almost perfect in France.**

sidered impolite to point with the fingers. Instead, they use pointed lips or their chins.

Authors Lennie Copeland and Lewis Griggs once asked an Englishman, "If it is impolite to point out someone, how do you do it without pointing?" Their companion dropped a shoulder, raised his eyebrows and jerked his head to the side, as though tossing it in the direction he meant to point. The authors said, "Clear as day, he pointed without pointing."

Extending the forefinger and little finger, like horns, while keeping the other fingers in a fist, was discussed in detail in Chapter 2 (see page 49). At the University of Texas, this represents the horns of a longhorn steer, the school symbol. Yet this same "horn" gesture in Italy signals that someone is being cuckolded. In some African countries, it is seen as casting a spell or a curse, and in Brazil it is an expression of good luck.

The *"V" for Victory* signal (index and middle fingers forming a **V** shape) is also discussed in Chapter 2 (see page 47). There you will learn its probable origins plus how this gesture and a 180-degree twist of the wrist can get you into a heap of trouble.

Rubbing the forefinger of one hand over the forefinger of the other hand is used in North America and recognized in parts of Europe to issue the reproof "Shame on you."

Waggling the forefinger back and forth is a fairly common and widespread gesture used to chastise someone, as if saying "No, no. Don't do that." The Japanese, however, expand on that and waggle the whole hand, palm outward, and in their case they are probably signaling "No, no. I am not worthy."

Crossing the fingers in North America and many parts of Europe is an expression of good luck and is probably derived from the cross of Christ (Figure 4.50). However, it is also done, usually in jest, when telling a white lie, as if making the sign of the cross defends and protects one from committing a sin.

Tapping the two forefingers together and side-by-side is a gesture that may be seen in places like Egypt. There it signifies "Would you like to go to bed with me?" (Figure 4.51).

Snapping the fingers may be a way of either getting someone's attention, or perhaps keeping time to music. But, snapping the fingers of *both* hands at the same time can have vulgar meanings in places like France and some Latin countries.

There are numerous and diverse gestures involving the fingers in connection with the head and face. These are described in earlier parts of this chapter, but here is a digest:

- *Tapping the temple with the forefinger* can either mean "intelligence" or "He (or she) is crazy."

FIGURE 4.50   In North America, "good luck."

- However, tapping the *center of the forehead* with the forefinger is, in the Netherlands, a way of silently saying "He's crazy."

- Taking the forefinger and pretending to screw it into the *temple* or the *cheek* is another way of sending messages. Italian men twist the forefinger into the *cheek* when they see a pretty girl. German auto drivers may be seen twisting the forefinger into the *temple* when some other driver has behaved badly; in fact, so strong a gesture is this in Germany that one can reputedly be arrested for doing it.

- *Kissing the fingertips* of the first three fingers is identified as a popular French gesture and signals a silent, graphic way of saying *"Magnifique!"*

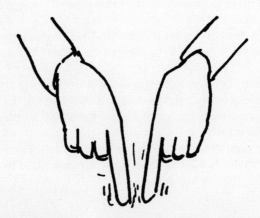

FIGURE 4.51   An Egyptian proposition.

- Lifting the hand up, palm out, making a fist, and extending the (1) thumb, (2) forefinger, and (3) little finger is shorthand in American Sign Language for the message "I love you!"

As a closing note to this segment on finger gestures, I once interviewed two retired Central Intelligence Agency operatives at a dinner party in Washington, D.C., asking if they knew of any unusual, unique gestures from around the world. Here is one story they related to me:

Sikhs are followers of a monotheistic religion founded in India and are distinguished by their colorful turbans and full beards. Today in New York City, many of them have taken up occupations as taxi drivers. If you should happen to employ a taxi driven by a Sikh, be watchful for one particular gesture. If traffic is heavy and tempers are fraying, watch to see if the Sikh *taps the face of his wristwatch* with his forefinger. If so, it has a special, almost ominous meaning to all those around. That simple gesture is a Sikh way of saying "It's twelve o'clock, and all Sikhs go mad at noon." In effect, it says ". . . watch your step. Check the time. It may be close to noon. That's when I go mad!"

LEGS AND FEET

"Putting your foot in your mouth" is just one of many ways to verbally offend someone using odd parts of the body. Here are other ways to offend when using the legs or feet.

Showing the sole of your shoe is a physical action that sends a rude message in many parts of the Middle East and Far East.

In one case, it even resulted in a murder (see page 8, Chapter 1). Specific places where this is offensive are Saudi Arabia, Egypt, Singapore, and Thailand. Since the sole of the shoe is obviously the lowest and dirtiest part of the body, it's not difficult to accept that in some cultures it is a mighty effective way to flash an insult.

In some of the countries just listed, it is also the custom to sit on cushions on the floor. As a result, some Westerners complain that "You have to be a contortionist to sit cross-legged on the floor and still not innocently point your sole at another person." Nonetheless, be careful. Watch how others do it. Keep your soles hidden by sitting on them or by tucking them underneath your knees.

In Thailand, *don't point with your toes*. There, the head is considered almost sacred and the foot is considered lowly and inferior. While it seems unreasonable that any of us might be in a situation where we would—or even could—point our toes at someone's head, in Thailand this would be the most grievous insult possible. The same applies to pointing your toes at a religious object.

Another taboo would be *putting up your feet on a desk* or any other piece of furniture. This taboo applies in many countries, including Thailand, Japan, and France. Once again, the symbolism here is that you are pointing the lowest part of your body at someone; or, in a milder form, you are showing disrespect by such an exhibition of casual informality.

Do you *cross your legs* when seated? Many people do. In fact, there are four distinct styles of sitting cross-legged. They are:

1. Legs crossed at the ankles,

2. Legs crossed at the knees,

3. One ankle resting on the knee of the other leg, and

4. Legs crossed at the knees and foot entwined around that same leg.

In some places, however, sitting cross-legged sends the wrong signals. In Thailand, it is considered so improper that a well-known Thai woman reformer and journalist was once physically removed from Parliament when she refused to uncross her legs.

In England (as noted in Chapter 1), what might be known as the "Royal Cross" consists of crossing the legs at the ankles, but not at the knees. Observe news photographs of English royalty, especially Queen Elizabeth II, and you'll see that Victorian primness prevails. She is almost always pictured with legs crossed at the ankles and never at the knees. Princess Diana, however, is often pictured with her legs crossed at the knees, proving that even royal conventions change.

In America, crossing the legs at the knee was at one time considered a somewhat effeminate posture, although it is very common now among both men and women. It is perhaps even more common among men in Europe. A second, more masculine cross-legged pose for American men is to rest the ankle of one leg on top of the knee of the other leg. Rarely would a woman be seen in such a position, unless she is wearing slacks.

A very feminine cross-legged pose occurs when a woman not only crosses the legs at the knees, but manages to also curl the upper foot around the calf of the lower leg in a virtual "figure eight." Men rarely, if ever, do it . . . maybe because they can't!

Whichever of these you prefer, be observant in the country you are visiting and consider following suit. In Japan, for instance, a solid and balanced sitting posture is the prevailing custom, so that it is probably

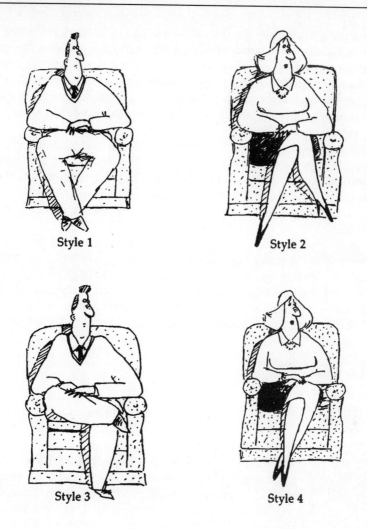

Style 1

Style 2

Style 3

Style 4

best to keep both feet planted squarely on the floor. And in the Middle East and parts of Southeast Asia, resting the ankle over the other knee risks pointing the sole of your shoe at another person, which, as we have already said, is considered a rude gesture in those regions.

In Japan it is often the custom to *remove one's shoes* before entering private homes, restaurants, inns, and tea and geisha houses. This practice is hard to miss, since you will not only see others removing their shoes, but you'll also quickly spot a row of shoes at the entrances—neatly arranged with toes pointing outward, away from the door. This is also the custom in Moslem countries. There, shoes are removed before entering some homes and always before entering mosques.

Even the *way we stand* can send messages. For example, standing with feet apart can be interpreted as being both aggressive and very masculine. A feminine posture, on the other hand, would have feet closer together and one toe pointed inward. Wide stances are regarded as masculine the world over, and narrow stances are considered feminine; women fashion models adopt narrow stances, while a husky male football player stands with feet planted wide.

Anyone who has served in the military is trained to stand with *heels together*, toes pointed out at a slight angle. As a result, this has become a posture that exhibits respect and attention in the presence of superiors. However, *clicking the heels* is no longer practiced except, perhaps, in parody of the Prussian signal for "At your service," where it seems to have originated.

Finally, perhaps you've wondered why, in the theater, performers tell one another to "break a leg." That odd expression comes to us from the English and means "good luck." It originated in Shakespearean times and means, "I hope you take a bow at the end of your performance." In the seventeenth century, to "break" the leg meant to bend at the knee, which is what one does when taking a bow before an appreciative audience.

FULL BODY

The feminine *curtsy* and the religious *genuflection* are probably two of the best-known gestures involving the full body. Moslems *kneel* at prayer and prostrate themselves with arms forward.

The male counterpart of the curtsy is the *bow*, but with the exception of Japan neither is commonplace or observed, except in the presence of true royalty. Even then, if anyone other than a British citizen should meet the Queen, proper decorum is for women to dip slightly and for men to bow the head downward slightly at the neck.

One signal involving the full body has been labeled *"mooning"* (Figure 4.52). It is seen in North America and has transited to parts of Europe. It is a rude gesture or joke that has actually become illegal in some countries. The person—usually a man—turns his back on the object of his derision, lowers his trousers to bare his derriere, and then bends forward to clearly expose his naked buttocks. Favorite settings for this gesture seem to be at sporting or musical events, in windows of moving cars, or from windows in dormitory or apartment buildings.

There are very few other full-body gestures that are considered acquired gestures and that vary from country to country. One fascinating, apparently instinctive full-body gesture is what Desmond Morris and other anthropologists have called "postural echo," something found in most societies. This refers to how friends who are conversing will often

FIGURE 4.52 "Mooning."

adopt similar body postures. This is usually not deliberate, scientists point out, but it happens frequently. If one person leans on a table with the elbows and tilts his/her head, the other person is likely to do the same.

Walking can reflect many characteristics of a culture. For example, Latin men who are friends may walk with arms linked. In Chapter 2 the segment on "Touching" (see page 39) describes cultures where men actually walk hand-in-hand.

In the Far East, notably in Japan and Korea, women customarily walk a pace or two behind male companions. Asian women often regard Western women as bold and aggressive, largely because Western women appear to walk with a longer gait and a more upright posture.

5

The Ultimate Gesture

If you are bewildered by the seemingly infinite number of gestures used around the world, and the nuances, shades of differences, and contradictions that separate them, perhaps this is the best point at which to introduce the "ultimate gesture." I call it that because it carries certain welcome characteristics unlike any other single gesture.

- First, this "ultimate gesture" is known everywhere—and I stress "everywhere"in the world. It is absolutely universal.

- Second, it is rarely misunderstood. Primitive tribes and world leaders alike know and use this gesture.

- Third, scientists believe this particular gesture actually releases chemicals called endorphins into the system that create a feeling of mild euphoria.

- Fourth, as you travel around the world, this gesture may help you slip out of the prickliest of difficult situations.

What is this singular signal, this miracle mien, this giant of all gestures?

It is, quite simply, the smile.

Use it freely. Use it often.

Having established that point, here are some little-known facts about the smile:

- *Some people are physically incapable of smiling.* There are eighty facial muscles that influence the smile. People suffering from certain forms of brain lesions, strokes, autism, or a rare nerve disorder called the Moebius syndrome are physically unable to smile because those muscles may be impaired.

- *Some people smile at strange times.* While living in Bangkok, American Richard Gesteland received the sad news that his mother had died. When he mentioned this to his Thai housekeeper, she greeted the news by smiling, even giggling. He later learned that in Thailand and other places such as Singapore, Malaysia, and the Philippines, people often *mask embarrassment* by smiling or even laughing. The Japanese are also noted for smiling when apologetic, confused, or even angry.

- *Some people are trained to not smile under certain conditions.* Norine Dresser, in her excellent book *Multicultural Manners* (Wiley, 1996),

documents several of these circumstances. The Japanese, for example, are conditioned not to smile for official government photos, such as for a driver's license, lest the occasion be considered too frivolous. Asian children new to the United States may hesitate to smile when photographed with Santa Claus or the Easter Bunny because this is considered a serious occasion. In the Korean culture, excessive smiling signals shallowness or thoughtlessness.

- *Finally, smiles come in many forms.* California psychologist Paul Ekman has cataloged fifty types of smiles. Fake or artificial smiles are often obvious, which is why actors must learn how to appear genuine when required to smile. Ekman explains that the way to tell a genuine smile from a fake smile is to look at the corner of the eyes. Look for the crinkle of skin at the corner of the eyes. A fake or polite smile uses the mouth only. And, of course, there is the "most famous smile" because it has had so many interpretations; it is the Mona Lisa smile.

6

The Innocent
Abroad's Shortlist

You are planning a trip overseas, or hosting an international visitor. When it comes to communications via gestures and body language, how can you separate *right* from *rude*, and *rude* from *crude*?

Here is a shortlist of the twenty gestures and examples of body language most commonly used by North Americans. To avoid misunderstandings, the single best piece of advice is to be observant and sensitive to what's going on around you. And don't be afraid to ask.

1. SHAKING HANDS

Here: When greeting one another, North Americans shake hands, and from an early age they are taught to do so with a firm, solid grip.

There: While hand-clasping as a greeting has generally been adopted around the world, the Japanese prefer to greet one another by bowing (but will quickly cater to Westerners by shaking hands). Southeast Asians press their own palms together in a praying motion. And when Middle Easterners and many Asians shake hands, they favor a *gentle* grip. That is because in their cultures a firm grip suggests aggressiveness.

2. EYE CONTACT

Here: When greeting and conversing with others, North American children are taught to look others directly in the eyes. To do otherwise is often regarded as a sign of shyness, or lack of warmth or—even worse—as weakness.

There: Japanese and Korean parents train their children to do just the opposite: *avert* the eyes and *avoid* direct eye contact. Direct eye contact is, to them, considered intimidating or may indicate sexual overtones.

3. WAVING

Here: Whether North Americans are signaling "hello" or "good-bye," or simply trying to get the attention of some distant person, they raise the arm and waggle the open hand back and forth.

There: Throughout much of Europe this action signals "No!" When bidding a greeting or farewell, Europeans customarily raise the arm and *bob the hand up and down at the wrist*, similar to the wrist action when dribbling a basketball. And Italians may use an entirely different version: palm *up*, fingers curling inward, back and forth.

4. BECKONING

Here: A North American will often summon another person by waving (to get their attention) and then turning the hand to make hand scoops inward. Another beckoning motion Americans might use is to raise the index finger (palm toward one's face) and make a *curling motion* with that finger.

There: Both of these beckoning gestures may be misunderstood in other parts of the world. Throughout Europe the gesture that means "Come here" is done by raising the arm, *palm facing down,* and then make a scratching motion with the fingers. As for the curling of the index finger, in places like Australia and Indonesia that is used only for beckoning *animals* and never for humans.

5. "V" FOR VICTORY

Here: Display the index and middle fingers in the shape of a V and virtually all over the world it is understood to mean "victory" or "peace."

There: Be careful, however, in England and Australia. There, when this same gesture is done with *the palm facing inward toward the face,* it is tantamount to signaling "Up yours!"

6. THE "O.K." GESTURE

Here: In a survey, this proved to be the single, best-known gesture in the United States with 98 percent recognition. North Americans flash this gesture frequently and enthusiastically: it's done by forming a circle with thumb and forefinger with the other three fingers splayed upward.

There: However, take care in France where this means "zero" or "worthless," or in Japan where it can mean "money," as if making the shape of a coin. In places like Brazil, Russia, and Germany, it is the signal for a very private bodily orifice. So in those countries, the American signal for "O.K." is definitely not.

7. THUMBS-UP

Here: North Americans and many other cultures flash this nearly ubiquitous gesture when they want to silently say "Good job!", "O.K.!", or "Great!" or a dozen other expressions, all of which demonstrate support and approval.

There: In certain locales, however, it can carry completely different meanings. In Australia, if the thumb is pumped up and down it is the equivalent of saying "Up yours!" Also, where North Americans may use the upright thumb when hitchhiking, in countries like Nigeria it is considered a rude gesture and should be avoided. In Japan and Germany, the upraised thumb is also used when counting: in Japan it signifies "five," but in Germany it is the signal for "one."

8. "HOOK 'EM HORNS"

Here: Most Texans will recognize this gesture (fist raised with index finger and little finger extended) as a University of Texas rallying call because it mimics the horns of the school's symbol and mascot, the famous Texas Longhorn steer.

There: But in Italy, this same gesture means someone is being cuckolded. In Africa, it can mean putting a curse on someone. And in Brazil and Venezuela, the same gesture is considered a good luck sign to ward off evil.

9. SPATIAL RELATIONSHIPS

Here: In normal social situations, North Americans generally stand about 30 inches apart from one another. That's considered the personal comfort zone and is equal to about an arm's length.

There: Asians, however, usually stand *farther* apart. In contrast, Latins and Middle Easterners stand *much closer*—sometimes even toe-to-toe, or side-to-side, brushing elbows. As a result, North Americans need to steel themselves for such close encounters because to move away sends an unfriendly message.

10. TOUCHING

Here: North Americans are not touch-oriented. With good friends, they may occasionally touch a forearm or elbow, and with *very* good friends they may go so far as placing an arm around a shoulder. But *hugging* is almost never done among casual acquaintances.

There: While Asians join Americans in shunning such bodily contact, Latins seem to dote on it with hearty embraces and warm pats on the back. In the Middle East, two Arab male friends may even be seen walking down the street hand-in-hand, and all it signifies is friendship.

11. KISSING

Here: Among North Americans, kissing is usually reserved for sweethearts, one's mother, and among close female relatives, but rarely between two men.

There: Among Latins, southern Europeans, and Russians, both male and female acquaintances will commonly greet one another with busses to the cheeks. These are more likely a feigned kiss to one cheek, sometimes both cheeks, and maybe even a "triple play": one cheek, the other cheek, and then back to the first cheek again. Incidentally, the continental practice of kissing a lady's hand has almost disappeared—except among a few pockets of gallants in Italy and other Romance-language cultures.

12. TOASTING

Here: North Americans will occasionally lift a ceremonial glass or clink the sides of glasses to toast others, but except for the best man at a wedding, that's about all that is involved.

There: Toasting is more common in other parts of the world. It is also often more elaborate, and more important. To avoid embarrassment, North Americans should first learn the local toasting customs in advance and carry along a short reper-toire of clever, all-purpose toasts to draw from on a moment's notice.

13. ENTERING A CROWDED AISLE OF SEATED PEOPLE

Here: At sporting events or the theater, North Americans usually slide into a crowded aisle while facing *forward*, with their backsides to the peo-ple already seated in that aisle.

There: In Russia and a scattering of other European countries, one enters an aisle *facing* the people already seated; to do otherwise is considered quite rude. To follow the correct local practice, just watch how others are doing it.

14. "I SEE A PRETTY GIRL"

Here: North Americans signal this message by wiggling the eyebrows up and down and perhaps whistling.

There: Italians convey this same message by screwing a stiff index finger into the cheek. Greeks stroke their chins, the French kiss their fingertips, and Brazilians form an imaginary telescope with their hands and then direct it at the object of beauty.

15. WHISTLING

Here: North Americans whistle at pretty women, but they also whistle as a form of cheering at sporting events and while applauding an outstand-ing performance. In these situations, it is a signal of approval.

There: Throughout Europe, however, whistling at such public events means just the opposite: a signal of disapproval, even derision.

16. NODDING AND SHAKING THE HEAD

Here: Throughout most of the world, nodding the head up and down sig-nifies "yes" and shaking it back and forth means "no."

There: In Bulgaria, however, the custom is just the opposite, especially among the older generation. There, to signal "no", they nod the head up and down, and to indicate "yes," they shake the head back and forth.

17. "YOU HAVE A TELEPHONE CALL"

Here: North Americans would probably send this signal by first forming a fist, then extending the thumb and little finger widely to simulate a telephone, and finally, holding it up to the ear. But this is not a universally understood signal.

There: In Argentina, for example, the accepted hand motion is to extend the forefinger and make a circular motion near the temple or ear—probably a vestige of the old hand-cranked telephones. (But to North Americans and Germans, this also is the signal for meaning "That's crazy!")

18. SIGNALING MEASUREMENTS

Here: Ask a North American "How long is six inches?" and he or she will probably hold out two stiff forefingers and separate them by an approximate distance of six inches.

There: In Colombia, however, using the forefingers in this manner is considered a very rude gesture. As a result, Colombians prefer a different system for gesturing both distances and heights. For distances, they will hold the hand and forearm out stiffly and take the cutting edge of the other palm to mark off the desired distance. For heights, holding the hand out with palm pointed downward is used to designate the height of *animals* only; to designate the height of a *human,* the palm is held vertically.

19. KNOCKING ON A DOOR

Here: In North American homes, bathroom doors are customarily left partially open. That way, we know it is not occupied.

There: In European homes, bathroom doors are customarily kept closed. Therefore, in European homes, always knock on the door first. One important footnote for Mexico: There you should avoid rapping on a door with the often-used "dum-de-de-dum-dum . . . dum-dum" (or rapping to the old musical phrase "Shave and a haircut, two bits"). In Mexico, this particular series of beats carries a very crude and rude message.

20. FINALLY, SLAPPING THE FIST UPWARD INTO THE OTHER PALM

Here: A North American might be seen idly swinging the arms while unconsciously slapping the fist of one hand into the palm of the other.

There: Be careful in Chile, however. This selfsame gesture has only one meaning, "Up yours!"

There you have twenty tips for knowing *right* from *rude*. Carry these with you and you can alter the appellation from "Innocent Abroad" to "Savant Abroad."

7

Country-by-Country Listing

Try this experiment: Sit in an international airport, tourist attraction, or cosmopolitan hotel and try to guess the nationalities of people passing by. Some are easy, while others are all but impossible. You may feel absolutely certain that fellow over there by the wall is Norwegian . . . but he turns out to be Greek.

The same play of clues and obstacles holds true with gestures and body language. Cataloging gestures around the world is like trying to catalog faces among the races of the world. There are the easy ones, the inconsistencies, and the surprises.

Even within a country, there may not be total agreement about the exact meaning of each gesture. For example, here is a typical comment from one cultural attaché when reviewing the listing for his country:

> There is no such thing as a universal attitude in my country on,
> for example, touching or not touching, and therefore [gestures]
> are hard to categorize. However, the common gestures you illus-
> trate are [known and understood].

So, as you read through this country-by-country listing, or as you hopscotch from one to another, bear in mind that these are the gestures in *general* use, but there may always be exceptions. Unfortunately, there is no definitive encyclopedia of gestures for all nationalities or countries. In fact, in my years of research, I came across only two countries (Brazil and the Netherlands) with reference books totally devoted to describing common gestures in use there.

If you are going to, say, Argentina, it might be a good idea to examine not only the gestures for that country but also to skim the list of common gestures for neighboring countries. Gestures cross borders easily, and this skimming process will help you get a feel for prevailing customs.

In the world of gestures, the best single piece of advice is to remember the two A's—"ask" and be "aware." If you see a motion or gesture that is new or confusing, *ask* a local person what it signifies. Then, during the rest of your visit, be *aware* of the many body signs and customs around you.

Use this topic of gestures as a gambit in conversation during your visit. When visiting another country, I frequently nudge social conversation toward the subject of gestures and body language. For example, one good conversational opener is, "What is the proper way to beckon a waiter in your country?" The response may be, "Oh, we gesture to a waiter this way. (Demonstrates.) But why?" Then you venture further: "I'm interested in different gestures and body language around the world. I'm interested in knowing what unusual gestures you have here in your country." Your companion will probably counter with, "Oh, we don't have any unusual gestures." But what they are really saying is that their gestures are not strange or unusual *to them*.

At this point, you can mention some of the oddities and anomalies around the world, such as the different interpretations given to the "O.K." sign, or the "V" for Victory sign. They'll catch on quickly. Best of all, they'll then want to know about "strange and unusual gestures" in *your* country.

Thus, the international communications gap narrows. Above all, remember that behavior is a fickle business. There are no absolutes. There is no single, comprehensive rule book for human behavior or nonverbal communication.

In summary, use the following listings as general guidelines . . . but also be "aware" and then, when in doubt, "ask."

EUROPE

Austria

- Shaking hands is the customary greeting, and it is done when meeting and leaving. A lady will often offer her hand in greeting, and it is polite to shake hands with the lady first, before the men who are also present.

- Handshakes will be firm, with direct eye contact.

- Austrian men may kiss a woman's hand when meeting. They may also enter a restaurant ahead of a woman—the purpose being to determine if the place is proper for a lady to enter.

- Men should rise when a woman enters the room.

- Prolonged touching, closeness, or backslapping are not common among new or casual acquaintances.

- Chewing gum in public is considered inappropriate.

- Hands in pockets when conversing should be avoided.

- Stroking an imaginary beard signifies that someone's comment is old and worn.

- Austrians keep the fork in the left hand when eating and push food onto it with the knife.

- Beckoning a waiter or some other person is done by simply raising the hand with the index finger extended.

- Keep your hands above the table when dining, with wrists or perhaps forearms resting on the table. Placing your hands in your lap during a meal is considered rude.

- Avoid cutting fish or potatoes with your knife; it suggests they are tough. A special fish knife is often provided when eating fish.

- Place your knife and fork side by side on your plate when you finish eating.

- To signify good luck, make two fists (thumbs tucked inside the fist) and gesture as if you are pounding lightly on a table.

- To signal "one," use the upright thumb.

- On highways, a rude German gesture may be seen in Austria in which the forefinger is twisted or screwed into the temple of the head. It means "You're a crazy driver!"

- Many of the gestures pictured in Chapter 2 are known in Austria. Examples: "O.K." sign, thumbs-up, forearm jerk, "the finger," and "V" for Victory.

Belgium

- Shaking hands is the common greeting, perhaps with a light pressure and briefly, not prolonged. If a woman wishes to shake hands, she will extend hers first.

- Handshakes are exchanged on both meeting and departing.

- When close friends meet, they may kiss cheeks. Remember, this is a *gesture*—not the real thing! No wet kisses. A light brushing of cheeks, a pursing of the lips—that's all. In Belgium, this is often done *three* times: (1) one cheek, (2) over to the other, and (3) back to the first.

- Pointing with the index finger is considered impolite.

- Snapping your fingers when others are present is also frowned upon.

- Standing with your hand or hands in your pockets while conversing is considered bad manners.

- Men allow women to enter rooms, board buses, and so on, in advance.

- Backslapping or being noisy is considered a rude action.

- When dining, keep your wrists on the table; don't place them in your lap.

- Belgians customarily eat Continental style—with the fork constantly in the left hand.

- Casualness may be regarded as rudeness. So, use good posture, never put your feet on chairs or tables, and yawning or scratching or using a toothpick in public are all considered poor manners. Same with blowing one's nose or sneezing—try to do them away from others.

- Many of the "Most Popular Gestures" described in Chapter 2 are known in Belgium.

Bulgaria

- The handshake is the customary form of greeting for both men and women.

- Bulgaria is much like the United States when it comes to touching and closeness. Physical contact is limited to such things as good male friends occasionally patting one another on the back, and good female or male-female friends greeting each other with the so-called cheek kiss, which is actually just a brushing of the cheeks.

- As in many European countries, it is the custom when dining to rest both wrists on the table. Exceptions will be seen in Bulgaria, depending on the individual and the setting, but a general practice is to not keep one or both hands in the lap.

- Except on formal occasions or when in the company of "good society," it's all right to sop up gravy with your bread, but use your fork rather than your fingers, of course. Avoid chewing loudly or making other unpleasant noises while eating.

- A rarity here is that nodding the head up and down means "no" instead of "yes" as in most parts of the world. Therefore, to say "yes," a Bulgarian will shake the head back and forth. Got it? (If so, shake your head back and forth—that means "yes.")

- Putting the forefinger to the temple and rotating it back and forth means someone is "crazy."

- As in most European countries, most of the gestures pictured and described in Chapter 2 will be known here, with these special notations: (1) the "forearm jerk" is a sexual insult but, in a way, it also means "You are not going to have your way as far as I'm concerned"; (2) the "V" for Victory can also be used to signal the number "two"; (3) the vertical or "hook 'em horns" gesture is not generally known; and (4) the "fig" is less of an insult and usually connotes "You are going to get nothing; I will not let you have your way."

The Czech Republic

- It's not uncommon in formal or informal settings, to do the round of shaking hands with everyone present on both arrival and departure. Follow the lead of your Czech colleagues.

- Czechs are not considered strong "touchers," except perhaps among artistic circles when casual acquaintances might hug when greeting.

- The hitchhiking gesture, using the upright thumb, is known, but to flag down an auto, a more commonly used motion is to wave the outstretched arm up and down.

- Never applaud in a church, whether the occasion is a wedding, concert, or whatever.

- Toasting is fairly common, but wait for the host to begin.

- As in Bulgaria and certain other countries, the signal to indicate something or someone is "crazy" is to take the stiff forefinger and "screw" it into the temple of the head.

- Czechs may not put their knife and fork down while eating, except of course when using a napkin or becoming involved in a lively dinner conversation.

- To signal you've finished eating, place the knife and fork in parallel at one side of the plate. To signal you're just pausing, place them in a criss-cross position on the plate.

- Avoid putting your elbows on the dining table at formal occasions.

- Czechs will be acquainted with most of the popular gestures shown and described in Chapter 2, but it's always worthwhile to inquire about any special nuances in their country.

Denmark

- A firm, fairly short handshake is customary. Children will often offer their hand in greeting and are taught to make direct eye contact and even bow slightly when meeting a hostess for the first time. When meeting a couple, shake hands with the woman first. If you are seated, be certain to rise to shake hands.

- Like most northern Europeans, Danes are friendly but not overly expressive physically.

- Politeness is very important. For example, going through a door is a ceremony in itself: women always go first, and men should allow their host to hold the door. Going up stairways, gentlemen always go first; down, ladies go first. At theaters, when entering the aisle, always face the people who are already seated.

- Formal dinners are fairly common in Denmark, so consider bringing appropriate clothes. Also, a card will be presented to each man with the name of the female dining partner who will be seated on his right. After being introduced to that woman, you should escort her to the table at the proper time.

- When going to restaurants, the man customarily takes charge. Waiters are signaled by simply raising the hand and index finger.

- Toasting is common and popular. Wait for the host to begin. Before sipping, look around at the group or toast one person directly, then sip and once again gain eye contact.

- Don't get up from the dining table until the host or hostess does.

- When driving, a gesture of contempt is to point the index finger at the temple and rotate it back and forth.

- Danes will recognize most of the more popular gestures described in Chapter 2.

England, Scotland, and Wales (Great Britain)

- Whereas on the European continent handshaking is done when meeting and departing, day in and day out and even with the same assortment of acquaintances, in these three countries it is done less frequently.

- Summon waiters at restaurants by raising the hand. To signal that you would like the check (called "the bill" there), make a motion with both hands as if you were signing your name on paper.

- In Scotland, unlike many European countries, eating on the street is considered acceptable.

- Loud conversations and any form of boisterousness in public places should be avoided.

- Avoid staring at someone in public. Privacy is highly valued and respected in these countries.

- The "queue," or line of people, is considered almost sacred. You must never "jump the queue," meaning to butt or push your way into a line of waiting people.

- In Wales, when addressing a group, speakers should avoid rubbing their noses, standing with hands in pockets, or shuffling the feet.

- In England, holding the nose and then pulling on an imaginary chain is a signal for "It stinks," and is something of an insult.

- Plan on meeting the Queen? Better be well prepared. When meeting royalty, the custom of bowing and curtsying is optional for outsiders. However, for men a slight inclination of the head would be appropriate and appreciated, and women should curtsy by slightly bending one knee. As for handshaking with royalty, the rule is that the first move will be made by them. Never actually touch the Queen, even to gently guide her in some direction. And don't offer to shake her hand unless she extends her hand to you first.

- If you smoke, it is the custom to offer cigarettes to others in your conversational group before lighting up.

- When drinking socially in British pubs, after paying for a drink, pick up your change. To leave it there (as is often the custom in the United States) could imply that you are leaving it as a tip.

- Other common practices: when yawning, cover the mouth; use handkerchiefs discreetly; remove hats when entering a building; men should cross their legs at the knees rather than placing one ankle across the other knee; women usually cross them at the ankles—in fact, watch for news photos of the Queen or other prominent women there and you'll note that when seated, they usually use the prim, Victorian manner of crossing them at the ankles.

- Most of the gestures in Chapter 2 will be known, but pay special attention to the "V" for Victory gesture. In these countries, it is done with the *palm facing outward;* to reverse the hand, with the palm facing yourself, signals "Up yours!" and is obviously rude and offensive.

- To repeat, politeness and good manners are expected and appreciated.

Finland

- The custom here is that both men and women will shake hands when introduced, or when meeting. Even children will often shake hands upon meeting guests.

- When greeting someone at a distance, a raised hand or tip of the hat is common. Also, men remove their hats when meeting or conversing, or when entering a home, church, or elevator.

- Bear hugs and cheek-kissing, so well known just across the border in Russia, are neither common nor popular in Finland. Emotions are not expressed publicly, only among relatives and very good friends.

- It is inappropriate to eat food while walking on the street. The only exception might be ice cream.

- The European style of eating—fork remaining in the left hand—prevails in Finland. Avoid eating anything with your fingers, including fruit.

- Refrain from eating before your host begins, and take small portions because it is the custom to eat everything on one's plate.

- When conversing, direct eye contact is important.

- Crossing the legs at the knees is preferred over crossing them ankle-at-the-knee.

- At a dinner party, it is customary to refrain from drinking until the host offers a toast, and to refrain from eating until the host begins.

- Standing with arms folded is sometimes viewed as a sign of arrogance.

- Always cover the mouth when yawning.

- Many of the gestures explained in Chapter 2 will be known in Finland, although not necessarily practiced.

France

- The mode of handshaking is usually as follows: a light, quick, single handshake, which is done with great frequency (arrivals, departures, each and every day). A strong, pumping handshake is considered uncultured. In general, the person of higher rank or status extends his or her hand first. Also, when entering a room, greet and shake hands with each person in the room. A French woman offers her hand first, except when the man she is greeting has a higher social or professional status.

- Close friends, family members, and young people often kiss on either cheek (but it is really *touching* cheeks and "kissing the air"). Depending on the region, it may be one, two, three, or four kisses on alternating cheeks.

- Be certain to carry a good supply of business cards, since they are exchanged often. In a formal setting, you may offer your card to a person of higher rank, but do not expect one in return.

- French body language and behavior are very restrained in professional settings. They gesture infrequently, but you can still read a great deal about them from their facial expressions. In social situations, the French gesture easily.

- Do not take off your jacket at a meeting unless the most senior person does so. Never, ever remove your shoes at a meeting or dinner.

- Some common actions and gestures to be avoided:

  — Resting the feet on tables or chairs

  — Using toothpicks, nail clippers, or combs in public

  — Conversing with hands in pockets

  — Chewing gum in public

  — Yawning, stretching, sniffling, or scratching in public

  — Holding loud conversations in public

  — Snapping the fingers of both hands, or slapping an open palm over the closed fist—both have vulgar meanings.

- The French refrain from smiling at strangers in public.

- It's not particularly polite in France to point with the hand and fingers, so when you want to beckon a waiter, it's best to make a discreet signal to your waiter by raising your hand slightly or nodding your head when she or he is looking at you. As you do this, just say "*monsieur*" or "*madame*" or simply say "*s'il vous plaît.*"

- To hail a taxi, many Parisians will snap their fingers as they raise their arm or wave their arm in front of them and yell "taxi."

- Never relax your posture in business settings or with people you don't know well. For example, don't slump back in your chair or extend your legs in front of you. Also, when seated, the French customarily cross the legs at the ankles. Good posture and decorum are virtues in France.

- Some unique gestures in France:

  — Forming a circle with your thumb and forefinger and placing it over your nose and then twisting; this signals that "someone is drunk."

— The "O.K." sign (thumb and forefinger forming a circle) in some parts of France signifies "zero" or "worthless."

— Here the "V" for Victory signal is done with palm *either* forward or backward; both mean "peace" or "victory." (In England, the "V" is *only* done with the palm outward; if the palm faces inward it is an obscene gesture.)

— Playing an imaginary flute is a way of signaling that someone is talking on and on and becoming tiresome. It also implies that you are not sure that the person is telling a true story. This is a rude gesture in a formal setting.

— On French highways, if another driver is not happy with your driving, he or she will pull alongside and glare at you.

• Always use a tissue or handkerchief when sneezing, and be as discreet as possible when blowing your nose. It is better to avoid sneezing in public. Try to stifle the sneeze, or if you cannot, turn away from others and say, "*Excusez-moi.*"

• When dining, the French use the Continental style, with fork constantly in the left hand. Also, rest your wrists lightly on the table and do not put your hands in your lap. Other dining practices:

— Bread or rolls are broken and eaten with the fingers and placed next to your dinner plate, usually directly on the tablecloth.

— At formal meals, fruit is peeled with a knife and eaten with a fork.

— Lettuce and other leaf vegetables are not cut with a knife but, instead, folded into small pieces and eaten with a fork.

— At family dinners it is O.K. to wipe up sauces with bread, but be cautious about doing so at formal meals. Follow the lead of your host.

— The French are sometimes uncomfortable picking up sandwiches, french fries, and other such foods with the fingers. It is more common to eat them with a knife and fork. (However, sandwiches made with crusty French bread may be eaten with the fingers because they are difficult to handle with a knife and fork.)

— When you have finished eating, place the knife and fork side-by-side across your plate with the fork tines up.

• When approaching the dining table, allow your host to indicate where you should sit.

- When using the hands to count, start with a fist, palm facing you, and then lift the thumb to signify "one," then add the index finger to signal "two," and so on.

- Author and Harvard professor Laurence Wylie also offers these important and singularly Gallic gestures:

  — Pointing to the eye means "You can't fool me."

  — To say "How dull," curl the fingers into the palm and rub the side of your jaw two or three times.

  — Using the index and middle fingers to push the nose upward signals "It's so easy I could do it with my fingers up my nose."

  — And when the French issue their famous shrug with the shoulders, palms extended, it means "It doesn't worry me." But if the palms are raised chest high, it becomes an emotional gesture, as in: "What do you expect me to do about it?"

- With the few variations just noted, the French will probably be acquainted with all the other popular gestures shown in Chapter 2.

As a final word on actions and physical behavior in France, just remember that the word *etiquette* is derived from French.

Germany

- A fairly firm handshake is the custom among men, often with just one or two "pumps." Children and women will often offer their hand in greeting, too. Public cheek-kissing is rare. It is done only at home among families and very close friends.

- Business cards are exchanged frequently.

- Shaking hands with the other hand in a pocket is considered impolite. For this reason, small children are chastised for putting their hands in their pockets because it is considered disrespectful.

- When arriving to meet a group of people, shake hands with each and every person.

- Men rise when a woman enters the room, or when they are conversing with a woman. However, this practice is seen less and less today. Women may remain seated when speaking to a man.

- Never open a closed door without knocking first.

- When acknowledging or signaling "thanks" to a crowd of people, Germans will often clasp their hands together and raise them high over their heads.

- During operas or concerts, it is important to remain quiet and still. Coughing or restlessness is considered rude.

- Men enter a restaurant *before* women, unless they are elderly or of higher status. One reason is, according to the custom, the man is inspecting the restaurant to see if it is proper for a woman to enter.

- When dining in some restaurants, if there are empty seats at your table and no other free tables, the maître d'hôtel may seat others with you. This is quite common in Germany—in fact, you can do the same if you arrive and there are no single free tables. There should be no obligation to carry on a conversation with others at the table unless both parties seem so inclined.

- Never place your foot or feet on furniture.

- At dinner parties, don't drink until your host or hostess begins. When toasting, clink glasses (wine only) before the first sip at both formal and informal occasions. Men toast women, never vice versa.

- When eating, the fork is held in the left hand; don't cut potatoes, pancakes, or dumplings with a knife because that suggests they are tough; rarely, if ever, eat with your fingers—that includes fruit and even sandwiches; hard rolls are often served at breakfast, and these can be cut with a knife or broken with the fingers.

- While eating, never rest one hand in your lap. You can, however, rest your wrists lightly on the table. Smoke between courses only if you see others doing so.

- A good general rule when eating is to watch and follow the actions of your German host.

- Chewing gum while conversing with another person is considered extremely impolite. As one German remarked, "To Germans it looks like a cow chewing on a cud."

- A man walks on the left side of a woman (Germans contend this is a romantic symbol because the heart is located on the left side), but on busy streets he will walk on the side where traffic is passing.

- To beckon a waiter, raise the hand with index finger extended and make eye contact with him or her.

- When waving good-bye, extend the hand upward, palm out, and wave the fingers up and down. Don't waggle the hand back and forth like a semaphore because that means "no."

- To signal for quiet, place the index finger over the lips, with fingernail facing outward.

- Four special gestures in Germany:

  — To signal "one," hold the thumb upright.

  — On Germany's famous autobahns (highways), if one driver is unhappy with the driving of another, he may point the index finger to the temple and make a twisting or screwing motion. This is considered *very* rude, and means, in effect, "You are crazy!"

  — To signal "good luck," Germans make two fists with thumbs tucked inside the other fingers and then make a motion as if they are pounding lightly on a surface.

  — In some parts of Germany, when people arrive at a large conference or dinner table and it is awkward to reach across and shake hands, they will simply rap their knuckles slightly on the table as a form of greeting to the others. The same gesture may apply when leaving the table ahead of the other guests. It is also used in university classrooms for students greeting professors.

- If you are driving or parking a car and you accidentally dent or scratch another car, *no matter how minor,* it is important that you contact the owner or even check with local authorities for proper procedures. Germans take great pride in their automobiles.

- Germans will probably recognize the common gestures described in Chapter 2, but make a special effort not to use the "O.K." gesture since it is considered very rude in Germany.

Greece

- The Greeks are warm and friendly, and handshaking will be the same with firm grasps and good eye contact the first and every time thereafter. You may even be embraced, with a kiss on each cheek, although men do this only after long absences. Good friends may also gently slap a hand on the other's shoulder.

- A slight upward nod of the head means "no." Another version is to lift the eyebrows upward. To indicate "yes" or "of course," the Greeks may tilt the head to either side or in an up-and-down motion.

- Greeks not only smile when they are happy but also sometimes when they are angry or upset.

- When you compliment a Greek, he or she may issue a puff of air through pursed lips which is an old action symbolizing the warding off of the "evil eye."

- Waving your hand palm outward and fingers spread is not a form of greeting. In fact, in Greece it can be confused with the Greek gesture *moutza*, where the hand is extended outward, away from the body, in something of a pushing motion. This is actually an ancient rude gesture still used today in Greece.

- Like many people in the Middle East and Mediterranean areas, Greeks may casually finger "worry beads." On first sight, these appear similar to rosary beads. But they have no special religious significance and are used more as an outlet for nervous energy or as a calming influence.

- When it comes to lines, or queues, in public places, the Greeks are the opposite of the British. Don't expect orderly lines.

- The "O.K." sign (index finger and thumb forming a circle) may be construed as a symbol for a body orifice, so use it with caution. It is rarely used to signify "O.K." Similarly, the "fig" gesture may be viewed as a phallic symbol, therefore obscene.

- To signal "everything is O.K.," use the thumbs-up gesture. However, the thumbs-*down* gesture is quite rude, the type of derisive signal you might see one bus driver flash to another when some rule of the road is broken.

- In Greece, the "middle finger up" is not generally known or used. However, as in Egypt and a few other Mediterranean countries, if you hold the hand out, palm down, and extend just the middle finger downward, *that* is an obscene gesture signaling "Up yours!"

- To express the sighting of a pretty woman, a Greek will use his hand and fingers to stroke his chin. A more forward, even crude, gesture is to hiss, wink, and make a kissing motion with the lips.

- To beckon someone, extend the arm, palm down, and make a scratching motion with the fingers.

- When dining, it is quite acceptable to use your fingers for the appetizers that are served before lunch or dinner. Also, Greeks may smoke cigarettes often during a meal.

- Male guests of honor usually sit to the right of the hostess, with female guests seated at the right of the host; whereas, say, in the Netherlands and Sweden the male sits to the left of the hostess and the female sits to the left of the host.

- At the dining table, the spoon placed above your place is for the dessert.

- Keep your wrists on the table while dining, not in your lap. As for which foods may be taken with the fingers, just watch your host and imitate him or her.

- To signal you have finished eating, cross your utensils in an X shape, knife under the fork. Another signal is to put your napkin next to your plate.

- Any visitor who participates in the Greek folk dancing is offering a gesture of appreciation and friendliness.

- Many of the gestures shown in Chapter 2 will be known to the Greeks but not necessarily used. For example, the "V" for Victory is known and used (and also means "We are *first*"), but the "hook 'em horns," "thumbs-up," and "middle finger" signals are not generally used. The "forearm jerk" is also known, but only because the Greeks see Europeans using it.

Hungary

- When initially meeting, departing, and upon meeting thereafter, the handshake is the customary gesture. A man usually waits for a woman to offer her hand.

- Hungarians are not considered a touching society. Two people usually stand about an arm's length apart.

- Embraces as greetings are uncommon and usually done only by good friends, maybe after long absences. Kisses are exchanged between female relatives and friends. It is uncommon for men to exchange kisses or have cheek-to-cheek contact with other men.

- At formal parties, wait to be introduced. At informal parties, introduce yourself.

- Men customarily walk to the left of women, or of any honored guest.

- Hungarians use their eating utensils in the Continental style: fork remaining in the left hand at all times.

- Keep both hands above the table, with neither one nor both in your lap.

- Many of the popular gestures shown in Chapter 2 will be known in Hungary, but it is best to check specific meanings with a local friend before using them freely. For example, the "V" for Victory is not common and the "fig" gesture signifies "You won't get (something)."

Ireland

- A relatively firm and straightforward handshake is the custom in both Northern Ireland and the Republic of Ireland.

- Business cards are not exchanged as formally as in other European countries.

- Physical contact is not common among those in Northern Ireland, except between very good friends.

- Also in the North, women are seated first. The more formal Irish will not cross their legs with one ankle over the knee but prefer instead to cross them at the ankles or one knee over the other knee.

- It's difficult to offend anyone in Ireland by innocently using the wrong fork or forgetting to shake hands at the right moment, so don't worry too much about it.

- One travel writer advises that the most offensive gesture in Ireland is failing to buy a round of drinks when it is your turn. Similarly, refusing a drink (except for health reasons) may be considered rude.

- Queues (lines of people) are common and respected, so don't barge into the middle of a line of waiting people.

- Generally, while the Irish have a worldwide reputation as being friendly, hearty people, they are not especially demonstrative with gestures or other body language.

- Most of the popular gestures shown in Chapter 2 will be known in Ireland, and especially the offensive reverse "V" for Victory gesture.

Italy

- Shake hands when meeting and departing.

- Italians are known for more physical contact than other Europeans: cheek-kissing among good acquaintances, embraces between men who are good friends, lingering handshakes with the other hand over your hand or at the elbow, and so on. You might also observe two Italian men walking along arm-in-arm.

- When visiting churches, women should not wear shorts or sleeveless or skimpy tops or blouses.

- In crowded public places, there are often no clearly visible queues.

- At the dining table, the host and hostess will usually sit at opposite ends of the table with the male guest of honor seated at the right of the hostess and the female guest at the right of the host.

- Your host should pour the wine, and Italians consider it unfeminine for a woman to pour wine.

- Although Italians drink wine every day with their meals, they seldom overimbibe. In fact, they drink wine for its taste more than its effects.

- Refrain from eating until your hostess begins.

- A knife and fork placed above your plate are used for dessert.

- Italians are known for being among the most demonstrative of all nationalities.

- It is best to cover the mouth when yawning.

- Shrugging the shoulders signals "I don't know" or "I don't care."

- Some specific hand gestures in Italy are these (full explanations are provided in Chapter 4):

  — The chin flick.

  — The "hook 'em horns," or *cornuto* signifies that your female mate has been unfaithful.

  — The "cheek screw," to denote seeing a pretty woman.

  — The "hand purse."

  — The "eyelid pull."

  — The "forearm jerk."

  — The "finger."

  — The "flat hand flick" means "I don't want it, get lost."

  — The "nose tap."

  — To wave good-bye, hold your palm up, fingers wagging up and down.

  — Tapping the hand to the forehead, like a salute, means "you're crazy."

  — "Throwing the saliva," or pulling imaginary saliva from the mouth and throwing it, is a strong insult.

- Be certain to also study all the popular gestures shown in Chapter 2, since most of these will apply—or be known—in Italy.

Netherlands

- Shaking hands always accompanies meetings and departures, for both men and woman. Children will shake hands, too. Embracing is done only among friends and relatives if they haven't seen one another in a long time or at times of bereavement. Women more commonly exchange kisses with close friends. Men do not exchange kisses with other men.

- Some unique gestures you may encounter in the Netherlands:

  — Bending the arm at the elbow, then tapping the underside of the elbow with your other hand signifies that another person is unreliable.

  — Grabbing at an imaginary fly in front of your face indicates that someone else is crazy.

  — If someone places a hand under their chin and draws it downward as if shaping a long beard, it is a way of saying "That story is very old."

  — The Dutch signal for "that person is crazy" is to tap the center of the forehead.

- Good, direct eye contact is important.

- Touching and other casual contact is not common, unless the parties are very close friends, and then there might be a slight embrace and even light kissing motions to each cheek.

- As in several other European countries, it is considered impolite to chew gum in front of others, or to stand with your hands in your pockets.

- When a man accompanies a woman walking along the street, it is the custom for men to walk on the side closest to the street.

- Among high society and the military, when a woman enters a room, the men usually rise.

- When dining, the hostess may serve herself first. Don't eat before the hostess.

- Take small portions of food, try to taste every item, and try to eat everything on your plate—not doing so may be considered impolite.

- The Dutch eat Continental style, fork in the left hand, and will eat even sandwiches and fruit with a knife and fork.

- Keep both wrists above or on the table, not in your lap.

- Getting up during a meal—even to go to the bathroom—is considered rude.

- Many of the Dutch will recognize the popular gestures shown in Chapter 2, so review these signals as well.

Norway

- Handshakes are fairly brief but firm, and little other personal touching is done here, except among relatives and very close friends. Avoid putting your arm around another person, or slapping him or her on the back.

- If you are seated, always rise to be introduced to another person.

- Avoid speaking in a loud voice.

- When dining, the host and hostess will sit at opposite ends of the table, with the female guest at the right of the host and the male guest at the left of the hostess. Don't start eating until your host or hostess does. The host will often give a brief welcome speech at the beginning of the meal. Norwegians eat Continental style, with the fork always in the left hand, and also use a knife and fork to eat the famous Scandinavian open-faced sandwiches. It is impolite to leave immediately after dining.

- Toasting is common: make eye contact, raise the glass upward to eye level, say "Skoal," drink, make eye contact again, and then place the glass down.

- To beckon a waiter, raise the hand with the index finger upward. Some young people may snap the fingers, but this is considered impolite.

- Most of the popular gestures shown in Chapter 2 will be generally known in Norway, but not necessarily practiced.

Poland

- Shake hands when you are introduced, when you meet someone for the first time that day, and upon departing. Men should wait for women to extend their hand first.

- An older Pole may very well lean down to kiss the hand of a woman, especially a married woman. Visitors are not expected to emulate them. Women greet close female friends with a brief embrace and slight kisses, one on each cheek.

- Poles are not considered "touchers," so hugs and embracing are not common, people usually stand about an arm's length from each other when conversing, and there is usually no other casual body contact (for example, touching when talking) except by very close friends.

- Poles tend to speak rather softly. Avoid chewing gum while conversing with another person.

- When dining, depending on the number of guests, the guest of honor is often seated at the head of the table. As in many European countries, when dining, the hands should be kept visible and above the table, never in the lap. Refrain from eating until all others have been served. Empty your glass only if you wish a refill.

- Toasting before and during the meal is very common. The host usually begins, and you can reciprocate later.

- When a Pole flicks his finger against his neck, he is inviting you to join him in a drink (usually vodka). This is a very common gesture, but used only among very close friends; otherwise it may be considered rude.

- Most of the gestures discussed in Chapter 2 will at least be recognized in Poland, but be aware which are used and what they mean. For example, the "V" for Victory signal is often seen in connection with the Solidarity labor movement. Also, whereas the "fig" gesture is considered obscene in places like Greece and elsewhere, in Poland it says, in effect, "In the end you will get nothing." Finally, the "hook 'em horns," or vertical horns, gesture is generally neither used nor known in Poland.

Portugal

- As in many Latin countries, a warm and firm handshake is the rule here. When close friends meet, shaking hands is not necessary; instead, men may pat or slap each other on the back, and women may embrace and kiss cheeks.

- The Portuguese are not overly demonstrative with hand gestures or body language.

- To wave or get someone's attention, the Portuguese will extend the arm upward, palm out, and wag the fingers up and down, as if patting someone on the head.

- To signal that everything is going well, the Portuguese use the thumbs-up gesture, sometimes using both hands (and thumbs).

- An unusual gesture in Portugal tells your hostess that you really enjoyed dinner. To do this, at the end of a meal kiss the side of your index finger and then pinch your earlobe between the kissed index finger and the thumb.

 • The "chin flick" has a different meaning than in Italy, where it shows impatience, even disgust. In Portugal, brushing your fingers (palm inward) off the bottom of your chin and away from your face signals "I don't know the answer." The same motion using the thumb means that something no longer exists, or something died.

- Portuguese eat holding the fork in the left hand at all times. To signal they have finished eating, they will place the knife and fork vertically on the plate. They rarely eat with their hands—even fruit is eaten with a knife and fork.

- Don't use bread or parts of a dinner roll to sop up gravy or juices. Before leaving the table, fold your napkin and place it beside your plate.

- As in other European countries, many of the more popular gestures explained and illustrated in Chapter 2 will be recognized in Portugal, although not all of them will be put to daily use.

Romania

- A traditional, firm handshake is the custom here but done frequently—on meeting, on departing, and even when meeting the same person several times in a short period of time.

- Men rise when meeting a woman; but the woman need not rise to be introduced.

- A Romanian man may lightly kiss the hand of a woman he is meeting, but outsiders should not feel obliged to adopt this custom. Very good friends and relatives will embrace and kiss cheeks.

- Business cards are freely exchanged.

- Women visiting a Greek Orthodox Church should dress conservatively, with bare arms covered and skirts rather than slacks. They need not cover their heads, however.

- When dining, several toasts will be exchanged. Romanians eat with the fork in the left hand, keep hands above the table, and keep the napkin alongside the plate rather than in the lap.

- Most of the popular gestures from Chapter 2 will be known, with two important notes: the "fig" gesture is a sexual insult and the "vertical horns" gesture signifies being cuckolded.

Russia (and the former USSR)

- A good, firm handshake along with direct eye contact is the customary greeting. In many parts of the old Soviet Union, among close friends the "Russian bear hug" is common and is often accompanied by three quick kisses to alternate cheeks—even among men—and sometimes with one kiss directly on the lips. There are exceptions to this practice, however. For example, in our survey of Uzbekistan, the reply was as brief as it was clear: "No kisses."

- Bear in mind that the old USSR was composed of fifteen very diverse republics with strong cultural differences. As a result, certain gestures and body language may have local flavors and meanings. For example, some of the new republics have Moslem cultural characteristics, so be certain to review some of those later in this book.

- At public gatherings, when people whistle, it is a signal of disagreement and disapproval. (Again, my respondent in Uzbekistan provided a cryptic footnote here that said: "Not now.")

- Another important taboo in public gatherings might occur in a theater. As you enter the aisle to occupy your seat, if you must pass in front of others, *always* turn and face them. Never pass in front of seated people in a theater with your back to them.

- The "O.K." sign is an ambiguous gesture here. While as an import from the West it is known to mean "O.K.," in some parts of the former Soviet Union it may be interpreted as a vulgar gesture.

- When entering or departing a Russian home, it is considered very bad form to shake hands across the threshold.

- Shaking the raised fist shows disagreement and anger. The thumbs-up sign signifies approval.

- When dining, Russians keep the fork in the left hand and the knife in the right. Also, keep your hands out of the lap while eating; instead, rest the wrists lightly on the table. However, research indicates this might be considered an old-fashioned practice in some parts.

- Russians count on their fingers from left to right, in a pattern opposite to American counting. Counting begins by bending the little finger and then the ring, middle, index fingers, and thumb toward the palm.

- When a Russian is annoyed with himself, he will slap his forehead with his flat hand and then turn his raised hand so the fingers are pointing down to the brow line, as if to say, "What a dummy—my brains are upside down."

- To indicate approval on a job well done, Russians will make a fist with the left hand, holding the thumb up straight (similar to the American thumbs-up gesture). The fingers of the right hand then rub together over the outstretched thumb in a sprinkling motion. This gesture indicates perfection, much like the fingertip kiss used in Western Europe.

- To beckon a waiter in a restaurant, a slight nod of the head should do the job; if not, just raise the hand and finger.

- Long, orderly lines of people are a common occurrence in daily lives, so be polite and respectful when joining one. Never butt into a line.

- People of the same sex often walk arm-in-arm in public. It is merely a sign of friendship.

- Visitors claim that the Russian people, especially in Moscow, do not seem to smile much in public gatherings or while walking along the street. On the other hand, in smaller private gatherings, the Russian people may be more open, more friendly, and may smile more often. Also, some Russians are not afraid to show emotions when in private situations. People of the same sex may be seen embracing, weeping, and kissing in these situations.

- Review the list of "most popular gestures" in Chapter 2. Most of these will be known, but not necessarily used daily, in the former USSR. For example, the "V" for Victory may be recognized as a Western gesture, but not used. The vertical horns (see page 49) may signify a curse, and the "fig" (see page 92) usually means "nothing," as in "You will get nothing" rather than the vulgar interpretation in Greece and other places.

Spain

- Handshakes are warm and friendly in Spain, often accompanied by a light pat on the back. As in many Latin countries, the *abrazo* (embrace) is common among male friends. Women do the same for male or female friends: a slight embrace, and the motion of kissing each cheek. Men and women always shake hands when meeting.

- Men usually wait for all women in a room to be seated before they sit down.

- Bringing the thumb together with the index and middle fingers in a rubbing motion means you are asking how much something costs or complaining about how expensive something is.

- Patting the cheek with the hand while looking at someone is how the Spanish convey that they think the other person has "some nerve." They will often say, *"Que cara!"* ("What nerve!")

- The Spanish always wait for everyone to be seated before they start eating. To do otherwise is considered extremely rude.

- Use your utensils for all foods, even sandwiches and french fries.

- To toast, everyone says *"chin chin"* and touches glasses.

- Never drink directly from a bottle when dining at a table.

- Whenever you see someone begin eating, you say *"buen provecho,"* which means "enjoy your meal."

- When seated before an audience, no matter how small, yawning or stretching is considered inappropriate. The same is true for taking off your shoes in public.

- When seated, Spanish men usually cross their legs at the knees; it is considered "unladylike" for women to cross their legs.

- Eye contact is important. But women should be wary of eye contact with strangers or new acquaintances since it signals interest. A Spaniard with "snapping eyes" is exhibiting either anger or impatience.

- The Spanish use many arm and head gestures. Hands should not be placed in the pockets when conversing, and gum chewing in public is considered rude.

- To beckon someone, stretch out the arm and hand, palm downward, and make a scratching motion toward your body with the fingers. Another way to call a waiter is to say "psssst," which locals may do but is considered somewhat rude if done by tourists.

- When dining, many special Continental customs apply: guests of honor are seated at the host's right; eating is done with the fork constantly in the left hand; never use your fingers to push food on to your utensils; keep your wrists on the table and avoid putting your hands in your lap; and to indicate you've finished eating, place the knife and fork in parallel across the plate—placing them on opposite sides of the plate can be interpreted as saying "I would like some more."

- Review Chapter 2, "The Most Popular Gestures," because many of these will be known and used in Spain.

Sweden

- As in other Nordic countries, handshaking is the common greeting, done with a firm grip and one or two pumps. For men, a slight nod of the head is customary when meeting for the first time and while shaking hands.

- No other touching is done, however, such as the bear hugs of Russia or the elbow touching associated with Latin countries. Swedes usually shake hands on arriving and departing and with every member of a group or family.

- For men and women, after greetings have been exchanged for the day, a slight nod when crossing paths is appropriate.

- Good eye contact when conversing is important. To Swedes, it is a sign that you are listening. Crossing your arms shows you are listening and is not considered a defensive posture.

- Body axis is almost parallel in Sweden. Angling away from a conversation partner is viewed as disinterest.

- Queues are respected, so avoid barging into the middle of a line of waiting people.

- Swedes are not physically demonstrative, and excessive gesturing is not common. Don't put your hands in your pockets when conversing with people.

- Smiling for no particular reason is considered superficial.

- When seated, men and women often cross their legs at the knees. Placing the ankle atop the other knee is considered rude in polite company.

- When dining, the male guest of honor is seated to the left of the hostess, and the female guest of honor to the right of the host.

- Toasting is done frequently in Sweden. The procedure is to lift your glass, make eye contact all around or with one particular person, say *"Skoal,"* drink, make eye contact again, and bring the glass to the table. The host makes the first toast.

- As a guest in a Swedish home, take off your shoes upon entering. Bring a lighter pair of shoes to change into if you do not care to walk around in your stocking feet. Do not put your street shoes back on until you are ready to leave.

- When leaving someone's home, wait until you get to the doorway to step outside before putting on your coat. To do so earlier suggests you are eager to leave.

- Swedes eat with the fork in the left hand, pushing morsels of food on to the back of the tines with the knife. Refrain from eating anything, including sandwiches, with your fingers.

- Behaviors Swedes find rude include interrupting people, leaving a conversation before it is concluded, and grooming yourself in public.

- Most of the popular gestures shown in Chapter 2 will be known in Sweden, but not all of them will be used.

Switzerland

- Since Switzerland is an amalgam of French, Italian, and German nationalities, customs from all three of those countries will be seen. For example, the German-type greeting tends to be shorter, firmer, and with no other body touching. The Italian and French influence will be seen when good friends add an embrace and even cheek-kissing. In all cases, though, shake hands with everyone present on arriving or departing and even with children.

- Presenting and exchanging business cards is an important custom, so carry a good supply.

- Good posture is considered an attribute in Switzerland. Crossing the legs is common, but not stretching them out; nor is slouching in your chair. However, when standing or waiting in line, be prepared for some amount of pushing and shoving.

- Be cautious about any form of littering. The Swiss take pride in tidiness and cleanliness, so any acts of littering are severely frowned upon.

- The Swiss are especially considerate about helping elderly people— alighting from buses, getting up to give them a seat, or helping them with luggage or other parcels.

- When dining, guests of honor are usually seated at the middle point of the table. Also when dining, keep your hands above the table, perhaps resting the wrists there.

- Don't smoke at the dinner table.

- A popular Swiss dish is *fondue*: a chafing dish containing melted cheese is placed in the center of the table and those around the table use long forks to dip pieces of bread into the cheese. One tradition is that if you drop your bread into the communal dish you must buy the wine; another version is that you must kiss all the members of the opposite sex at the table.

- As in Germany, when dining in a restaurant, don't be surprised if strangers approach and seat themselves at unused seats at your table. It is not necessary to strike up a conversation, incidentally.

- Most of the popular gestures described in Chapter 2 will be known— although not all of them necessarily practiced.

Turkey

- The standard handshake applies here, but old friends may also clasp both hands over yours or even embrace while kissing both cheeks. On arriving at an office or other gathering, shake hands with each and every person. If a person is much younger than you, he may kiss your hand and press it to his forehead.

- Inadvertently pointing the sole of your shoe toward someone is an insult. Therefore, be careful in any sitting position. For example, never lean back in your chair and put your feet on a desk or table. That would be considered a gross sign of disrespect.

- Ask permission before smoking, but it is considered impolite to smoke or eat while on public streets.

- Show respect to elders. Speaking in a loud voice to elders—and to others—is considered ill-mannered. Always stand when an elderly person enters the room.

- The "fig" gesture with hand clenched in a fist and the thumb protruding between the first two fingers is a rude gesture in Turkey.

- A gesture unique to Turkey is a way of signaling that "something tastes good." It is done by holding the hand up, palm upward, and bringing the fingers into the thumb, in a grasping motion, then shaking the hand.

- Men in Turkey will be seen holding and fingering loops of beads. These are called "worry beads," used for relieving tension or as a sign of manhood; they often have no special religious significance.

- Raising the head slightly, tipping it backward, and closing the eyes usually means "no" in Turkey. "No" can also be expressed by opening the eyes wide, raising the eyebrows, and tipping the head backward.

- When Turks want to tell you to "forget it" or "don't worry," they hold the hand, palm upward, with a bent elbow; from this position, they sweep the hand upward as if throwing something over their shoulder.

- It is considered rude to cross your arms over your chest while conversing with someone. The same is true of putting your hands in your pockets.

- Remove your shoes when entering a Turkish mosque, and most Turkish homes.

- Signs of affection—hugging, holding hands, kissing—are usually not done in public. It is common, however, especially in rural areas, for people who are casual acquaintances to kiss one another when meeting and parting.

- Turkish women in small towns will usually not engage in casual conversation with a man until they have been formally introduced.

- Before taking photographs, ask permission—especially in mosques or of individuals.

- The "tch" sound means "no" in Turkey.

- When dining, Turks keep the fork in the left hand and push food on to it with the knife. Avoid eating with the fingers. If you are offered a toothpick after dining, it is O.K. to use it, but be certain to cover your mouth with the other hand.

- To politely decline an offer of food, put your hand over your heart while tilting your head back slightly.

- Among the popular gestures described in Chapter 2, here are the pertinent interpretations in Turkey: the "forearm jerk" (pages 32–33) implies strength rather than a sexual insult; the "V" signal tends to mean "two" rather than "victory"; the "O.K." circle made with thumb and forefinger signifies homosexuality; the thumbs-up gesture means "O.K."; and the vertical "hook 'em horns" (page 49) gesture is not generally known or used.

Yugoslavia (former)

Since the first edition, Yugoslavia has broken into six nations: Bosnia-Herzegovina, Croatia, Macedonia, Montenegro, Serbia, and Slovenia. At this writing, the U.S. State Department advises against travel in certain regions of all countries except Slovenia and Macedonia. The latter are the only two countries unaffected by civil conflict; however, Macedonia is the poorest of the six republics, making it an unlikely business destination for North Americans.

The following information will apply generally across all republics.

- A firm handshake is the custom for both sexes, although a man should wait for the woman to extend her hand first. Close friends and relatives will greet one another with slight embraces and kisses on the cheeks. Even when staying in a private home, you may find that people will shake your hand each morning and evening.

- It is best to dress conservatively, especially women.

- The "O.K." sign means something is "perfect" or "exact" or "it's super."

- The "fig" gesture is *not* considered especially rude, as in some other Mediterranean countries. Here it symbolizes "zero" or "nothing," as when a parent might signal to a child, "No, you may not have any ice cream."

- The thumbs-up gesture means "O.K." and is also commonly used for hitchhiking.

- Forming a fist and holding it head-high can have two meanings. If the fingers are shown outward (as in the Black Power gesture), it means "Victory!" However, if the knuckles on the back of the hand point outward, it is a gesture showing strong anger and signals "Up yours!"

- Two common gestures described and pictured in this book should be avoided in the former Yugoslavia because they could be interpreted as rude, even obscene. The "hook 'em horns" gesture means "Up yours," especially when the fingers point toward the person in question. The second one involves slapping the palm of one hand downward on top of the fist of the other hand.

- Another obscene, gesture found in some Mediterranean countries is known and used in the former Yugoslavia. This is when a person holds his hand out, palm down, and extends the middle finger downward.

- The "forearm jerk," as in many countries, means "Up yours!" but for added emphasis a person may not only hit the crook of his bent elbow but the shoulder as well.

- The "eyelid pull" means "nothing," as when one tour guide might signal to another "I received no tip."

- The "hand purse," so common in Italy, is known in the former Yugoslavia to mean "it's good," as when conveying, "This food is so good."

- To beckon a waiter, merely raise your hand. But never beckon a person by using the index finger in a curling motion. That is used only to beckon animals.

- The middle finger extended is not generally used or known in the former Yugoslavia.

- When dining, it is the custom here to keep the fork in the left hand at all times, pushing the food on to it using the knife.

- To indicate you have finished eating, place the knife and fork across the center of the plate.

162   GESTURES

- Keep both wrists on or above the table while eating; it is not considered polite to place one or both hands in the lap, as is the custom in
  the United States and certain other countries.

- Women visitors should avoid making eye contact with or smiling at
  strange men while walking in public.

- Many of the gestures shown in Chapter 2 will be known and recognized, but with the exceptions and variations in meaning just
  explained.

MIDDLE EAST AND AFRICA

Gestures throughout the vast African continent and the culturally complex Middle East vary because of the huge distances and many different
nationalities residing there. Nonetheless, here are some general guidelines for the most heavily visited countries. This listing provides key gestures and body language as a foundation to learning more as you visit
these countries.

The Arab World

The so-called Arab World consists of about twenty countries stretching
from Mauritania in the west to Oman in the east. Within that area is a
diverse group of people bound together primarily by language and religion—and, some would add, by oil. While religion is a strong common
denominator, adherence ranges from very strict and fundamentalist to
very loose and liberal. The same spectrum applies to gestures and body
language: some rules and actions are adhered to strictly, others less so.
   Some general customs one might observe when visiting this region
include:

- Sit properly, without slouching or putting feet up on a table or other
  furniture. When standing and conversing, avoid leaning against a
  wall or standing with your hands in your pockets; both are considered disrespectful.

- Avoid showing the sole of the shoe, or inadvertently pointing it at
  someone. The shoe soles are the lowest and dirtiest part of the body,
  and therefore it is rude to point them at someone.

- Arab men will be seen fingering loops of beads that resemble a
  Catholic rosary. But for Arabs, many of whom are Muslim, these are

tension relievers called "worry beads" and have little or no religious significance.

- The right hand prevails: eat with it, present gifts with it, touch with it. The left hand is generally regarded as the "unclean" hand and is used primarily for bodily hygiene.

- Shaking hands is important, although the grip may be less firm than Europeans and Americans use.

- Arab males are considered a "touching society." Handshakes may be prolonged, elbows may be grasped, and two men may even hold hands while walking on the street.

- When two men converse, they will probably stand much closer than Westerners. On the other hand, men should not touch an Arabic woman unless she extends her hand first.

- Long, direct eye contact among men is important. In fact, staring is not necessarily considered rude or impolite.

- People should not be photographed without their permission.

- Public displays of affection are frowned upon.

- Gesturing "no" is often done by tilting the head backward and either raising the eyebrows, jutting out the chin, or making a clicking sound with the tongue.

- The thumbs-up gesture usually means "Very good. I am winning."

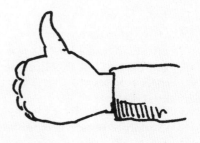

- Keep household pets away from visiting Arabs. Most Arabs do not like to be touched by or be in the presence of such pets, especially dogs.

Some specific comments for specific Middle Eastern and African nations follow.

Congo (formerly Zaire)

- As in many African nations, the large number of tribal cultures causes a great diversity in social customs. However, in the capital city of Kinshasa, the handshake is the appropriate greeting for visitors.

- There is minimal public contact between men and women.

- Dining is an important social custom here, and one is often judged by one's conduct while eating.

- If your host uses the fingers to eat, do the same but use only the right hand.

Egypt

- Handshakes are customary, but perhaps not with as firm a grip as Americans and Europeans use. Greetings will be warm and expressive because Egyptians believe personal relationships are important.

- Spatial relationships among males will be closer than Americans and Europeans are accustomed to. They will tend to stand close, and moving away may be misinterpreted as aloofness. In contrast, people of the opposite sex stand farther apart than in the United States or Europe.

- Men tend to be more touch-oriented as well, and therefore a handshake may be accompanied by a gentle touching of your elbow with the other hand.

- The right hand only should be used for eating. Throughout most of the Middle East, it is the custom to reserve the left hand for bodily hygiene.

- Many Middle Easterners have what Americans and Europeans consider "languid eyes." It appears to many outsiders that the eyelids are half closed, but this does *not* necessarily signal disinterest or disrespect.

- It is best not to sit cross-legged, because showing the sole of your shoe to another person is considered an insult.

- Many Egyptian husbands and wives walk together hand-in-hand. However, some husbands observe the tradition of walking slightly ahead of their wives.

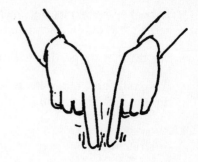

- Tapping the two index fingers together (side-by-side) means "let us be together," but is sometimes interpreted as "let's sleep together."

- Smoking in public places is very common, and it is polite to offer cigarettes from your pocket to others present.

- When dining, it is preferable to eat everything on your plate.

- Western eating habits prevail here—most foods are eaten with a knife, fork, or spoon. When in doubt, follow the lead of your host.

Ghana

- Western-style greetings are known and used here, but this country is composed of many different ethnic groups, each with its own distinct language, customs, and culture.

- Children are trained not to look adults in the eye since this is considered an act of defiance.

- When eating, Western etiquette is practiced in Ghana.

Iran

- Handshaking is the customary form of greeting. As in most of the Arab nations; however, it may be done with a lighter grip. Good friends may greet each other with a slight embrace and a gesture of cheek-kissing.

- People of the same sex will tend to stand close together when meeting and conversing.

- Shaking hands with a child shows respect for his parents.

- When entering homes, especially rooms with carpets, it may be the custom to remove one's shoes first. Always remove your shoes before entering a mosque.

- Men and women rarely exhibit any signs of affection in public.

- To beckon someone, put the hand out, palm down, and curl the fingers in and out in a scratching motion.

- The thumbs-up gesture is considered vulgar.

- To signal "no," move the head up and back sharply. To signal "yes," dip the head downward with a slight twist.

- Avoid blowing your nose in public. Refrain from slouching in a chair or stretching your legs out in front of you. Also, watch where you point the sole of your shoe, which is considered offensive to anyone seeing it.

Israel

- Warm handshakes are the custom here, and good friends will accompany the handshake with friendly pats to the shoulders or back. Israelis do not usually embrace or hug when meeting unless they are very close friends.

- Israelis have small "personal bubbles," meaning they stand close to one another and there is little concern for invading someone else's "space." Moving back is considered rude, and you will be seen as being standoffish.

- Israelis use direct eye contact, as in North America.

- Some Israelis are very expressive with hands and bodies, and others are more reserved and sedate.

- To Westerners, Hebrew seems a very loud and expressive language, and men often touch each other on the arm while talking to get their point across. Touching is common between friends; in fact, if an Israeli holds your hand, it is a sign of friendship. You may see more touching between Israeli men than you would see in North America.

- Be aware, however, that there are many Arabs living in Israel who practice their forms of body language: no casual touching, conservative dress, no direct eye contact with women, and so on.

- Women should not initiate physical contact. Wait for the Israeli to extend his hand. If he doesn't extend his hand, nod your head as a greeting. This is very important among Arab Israelis who may not be able to touch women because of religious laws.

- Also, when dealing with Orthodox Jews, both men and women should avoid casual touching or handshaking with the opposite sex. It is permissible to pass business cards in a normal fashion, but try to avoid actual physical contact.

- Visiting women should avoid casual smiling among strangers, especially in public places, because this is not common and may be misinterpreted.

- Western-style eating etiquette is practiced throughout Israel.

- An Israeli insult is to point down at the upturned palm of one hand with the forefinger of the other hand, implying that "grass will grow on my hand" before the speaker's comments come true.

- Bringing together the thumb and other four fingers in an up/down motion means "slow down."

- All of the popular gestures described in Chapter 2 are known in Israel: The "O.K." sign with thumb and forefinger means just that and is not considered vulgar; "thumbs-up" means "O.K."; the extended middle finger is a sexual comment; the "V" means "victory"; and so on.

Jordan

- Both friends and strangers are greeted warmly, with sincere handshaking. Long acquaintances of the same sex may embrace lightly and kiss either cheek.

- Among the elderly and more traditional, the *salaam* greeting may be used. That is done by taking the right hand, touching the heart, then the forehead, and then gesturing forward. The verbal expression is *salaam alaykum*, or "peace be with you."

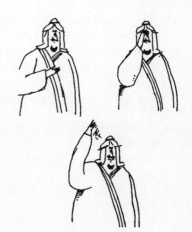

- Guests are always warmly received.

- When dining, it is the custom to refuse offers of additional food at least two times, then accept on the third offer if you actually wish more.

- It is polite to leave small portions of food on your plate.

- Coffee in the Middle East is often what Westerners consider thick, syrupy, and strong. It is customarily served in small cups, refilling them often. If, as a visitor, you wish to signal "no more refills," just tip the cup back and forth with your fingers.

- As in other Arab countries, it is impolite to point the sole of your shoe toward another person.

- When crossing the legs, it is the custom here to cross them at the ankles or the knees, but not to place one ankle on the other knee.

Kenya

- The most common physical greeting is the conventional handshake as imported by British colonizers. However, members of some local tribes may greet one another by gently slapping palms and then gripping each other's cupped fingers.

- Using the left hand to receive a gift is considered impolite.

- Take care when photographing local residents; it is best to ask permission in advance.

- Many of the gestures and body language from Britain are known and used in Kenya.

Lebanon

- The handshake is the customary greeting, often accompanied by a courteous nod of the head. Also, since many cultures in the Middle East are more touch-oriented, a Lebanese male may touch your arm or pat you on the back as a signal of friendship. Close friends may lightly embrace and kiss each other on the cheeks. Men may tip their hat when greeting a woman.

- As in many Middle Eastern countries, personal space is smaller than in most Western countries. Therefore, people of the same sex tend to stand closer together.

- Children are usually taught to refrain from speaking unless spoken to by visitors.

- Posture is considered important in Lebanon, and gestures and bodily expressiveness are freely used.

- While signaling "yes" is done with a nod, to signal "no" a Lebanese may perform a sharp upward motion of the head accompanied by raised eyebrows.

- To beckon someone, the proper gesture is palm down, fingers curling in and out in something of a scratching motion.

- It is impolite to show the sole of your shoe to others.

- A gesture that signals "no" is raising the hand, palm outward toward the other person.

- A closed fist raised up into the air is regarded as a rude gesture.

- The following is considered an insulting gesture: hand up, palm outward, fingers spread, drop the middle finger, and hold it down with the thumb.

- Licking the little finger and then brushing it across the eyebrow is a signal that someone is homosexual.

- Many Lebanese men carry "worry beads" that resemble a Catholic rosary but have no special religious significance. They are simply stress-relievers; you will see the men fingering and twisting these beads on the street while walking, while seated, during business meetings, and on all types of occasions.

Mali

- The handshake is common and often done with the left hand touching the other person's elbow as well. Many other forms of greetings will be found due to the ethnic diversity in Mali.

- Men shake hands with women only if women offer their hand first.

- The northwestern part of Mali is influenced by Islamic customs, so many of the gestures and body language used in the Arab region will apply there.

- Watch your host for clues and direction, but it is customary to remove one's shoes before entering a room.

Morocco

- Greetings are important in Morocco and come in different forms. In the larger cities, good friends will greet by brushing or kissing cheeks.

Multiple kissing implies even closer ties and sincerity. In rural areas, handshakes are often accompanied by touching the heart with the right hand and then kissing the forefinger joined to the thumb.

- When dining, the host may bring water and a basin for guests to wash their hands. At Moroccan-style meals, diners sit cross-legged on the floor at low tables. Remove your shoes before being seated.

- It is quite acceptable—common, in fact—to eat with the fingers from a common platter of food. But use the right hand only. Follow the actions of the host.

- Common Arab practices prevail here, such as not showing the sole of the shoe, occasional absences by hosts to attend prayers, and so on.

Nigeria

- Because of diverse cultures in Nigeria, it is difficult to generalize about proper greetings. However, those who travel there as tourists or on business will probably find that the local people they deal with know and use Western conventions.

- Nigerians try very hard to please guests. They are congenial and hospitable and respect the Western regard for punctuality.

- Among one major ethnic group, the Yorubas, an important guest will be greeted by applause.

- Members of the same sex will stand closer together than most Westerners normally do.

- One vulgar gesture that should be avoided is the "hand push," where the hand is held forward at shoulder or head level, with the fingers spread.

- Avoid pointing the sole of the shoe or foot at a person.

- Use only the right hand for eating finger foods.

- The Yorubas will wink at their children if they want them to leave the room.

Saudi Arabia

- Men will greet each other with a light but sincere handshake, sometimes with the left hand touching the forearm, the elbow, or even the shoulder of the other person.

- A Saudi man accompanied by a veiled woman will probably not introduce her.

- Among Saudi males, an embrace and cheek-kissing may be added to their greeting.

- As in other parts of the Middle East, among the elderly and more traditional folk, the *salaam* greeting after the handshake may be observed. This is done by using the right hand to touch the heart. It is accompanied by saying *salaam alaykum* or "peace be with you."

- Saudis may signal "yes" by nodding the head up and down. "No" is indicated by tipping the head backward and clicking the tongue.

- In the central region of the country, Saudis will touch noses when meeting people from their tribe.

- At political gatherings, it is not uncommon to see men greet elders and dignitaries by kissing their right front shoulder.

- Spatial relationships are smaller by Western standards. People of the same sex will stand closer together than North Americans or Europeans do.

- While walking along a street or in a corridor, a Saudi host may guide a Western male by gently holding his elbow or even taking his hand and continuing to walk along hand-in-hand. This is a sign of friendship and respect.

- Many Saudis have been educated in the West or have carefully learned Western ways, so they will be well acquainted with Western customs. Therefore, you may receive a firm handshake, no touching, larger spaces, and so on.

- Avoid excessive amounts of pointing or signaling with the hands.

- Joint meetings may be encountered—that is, different groups of business visitors may be seated in separate parts of the same room, with the Saudi host moving from one group to another.

- Your Saudi host may interrupt a meeting or conversation, leave the room, and be gone for fifteen or twenty minutes. This usually signifies he has gone to conduct his daily prayers.

- Women are not permitted to drive vehicles.

- Eye contact is important. The saying that "the eyes are the windows to the soul" applies here. Many Westerners observe that Middle

Eastern men seem to have "languid" eyes and misinterpret this as boredom or disinterest, which is not necessarily true.

- In this area of the world, the left hand is customarily used for bodily hygiene. Therefore, it should *not* be used for eating, handing over gifts or business cards, or other such gestures.

- Crossing the legs in front of non-Westernized Saudis may be taken as a sign of disrespect. The same applies to putting your foot or feet up on a piece of furniture.

- Any time you put the middle finger out—whether pointing up or down—it is considered vulgar.

- Avoid showing the sole of your shoe to another person—it can be considered an insult since the sole is the lowest and probably dirtiest part of the body.

- Take your shoes off before entering a room.

- Any display of more intimate areas of the body is disliked; this includes bare shoulders, stomach, and calves and thighs.

- The "worry beads" so common throughout the Middle East will be seen often in Saudi Arabia. This is a string of beads resembling a Catholic rosary but carrying no similar religious meaning. They are fondled strictly for personal relaxation.

- Smoking of cigarettes in public is not common. However, in some Saudi locations the communal water pipe, or *hookah*, may be passed around among those present.

South Africa

- Since this country is an amalgam of black African tribal, Dutch, and English cultures, influences of each can be found. The handshake is still the commonly accepted form of greeting for most visitors.

- Refer to sections in this listing for the Netherlands and for England for gestures commonly known and used there. Many of these will be known and used by the white population in South Africa.

- The raised right-handed fist has become a world-recognized symbol for Black Power. In 1990, it received international publicity when South African black leader Nelson Mandela toured Europe and North America.

- Visitors to South African international airports report that porters will approach them with both hands held out in a cupped shape. At first glance, it appears they are begging for a tip, but it is reportedly a signal of humbleness or of supplications, saying, in effect, "The gift you may give me (for carrying your bags) will mean so much that I must hold it in two hands."

- The Continental style of eating prevails among the white population and many of the blacks. Also, cover the mouth when yawning.

Sudan

- In the North, where Arabic customs prevail, greetings consist of a warm but gentle handshake. Good friends of the same sex may embrace. But men should not take the initiative to shake hands with a woman unless she extends her hand first. In fact, men should not publicly touch a woman.

- As in other Arabic-influenced countries, the left hand has limited use: its role is for bodily hygiene. The right hand should be used for greetings, for eating, for handing over business cards or gifts, and for gesturing. Pointing with the finger may be considered rude.

- Avoid showing the bottom of your shoe to another person; this is considered rude.

- The Arabic language is considered by some a dramatic and emotional language, and conversation is often vigorous and enthusiastic.

Tanzania

- Among the Swahili-speaking coastal population, the handshake is the customary greeting. Local men do not normally shake hands publicly with women, but foreign visitors are often excused for doing so.

- Avoid using the left hand when giving or receiving a business card, gift, envelope, or such.

- Otherwise, most European gestures are known.

Zambia

- The handshake is the accepted greeting here, with possibly the added feature of the left hand supporting the right. This demonstrates respect.

- Among local inhabitants, kneeling before the elderly or social superiors may be observed.

- Among some tribes, gentle thumb-squeezing may be practiced, along with clapping.

- People of the opposite sex rarely have physical contact when greeting.

- Direct eye contact between sexes should be kept to a minimum lest it suggest romantic interests.

- Pointing one's finger at someone is considered improper. It is acceptable to point discreetly at inanimate objects.

- Wash hands before and after eating because the right hand is often used to pick up food from a common bowl or dish. Public spitting is considered a sign of disrespect.

Zimbabwe

- The handshake is the safe, accepted, and common form of greeting. Local women and girls may even curtsy.

- In rural areas men often remove their hat when greeting an elderly man or woman.

- An older tradition is to give—or accept—a gift using both hands.

- Often a signal of thanks and politeness is shown by clapping the hands.

- Avoid long, direct eye contact. This is considered somewhat rude, especially in rural areas.

- The young are discouraged from talking to elder with their hands in their pockets.

PACIFIC AND ASIA

Australia

- A firm, friendly handshake is the customary greeting here. It's not necessary, though, to offer to shake hands with a woman unless she offers her hand first. Women friends may kiss when greeting each other. When greeting someone at a distance, a wave is customary but yelling is not.

- Be prepared to exchange business cards, but this practice is not as rigid as in, say, Japan or some European countries.

- In business meetings, eye contact is important.

- When addressing audiences, use erect posture and modest gestures.

- Australian men do not consider it good form to show much emotion, so good friends may pat one another on the back, but there is not much physical expressiveness of emotion beyond that. It is considered unmanly.

- Even if you are friends, winking at a woman is considered rude.

- The thumbs-up gesture is considered a rude and improper gesture, especially when jerked upward.

- Guests of honor usually sit at the right of the host. Eating is done in the so-called Continental style—that is, with the fork held constantly in the left hand and the knife in the right. When eating soup, move the spoon away from you and not toward you. To indicate you have finished eating, lay the knife and fork in parallel on your plate. While eating, keep your elbows off the table.

- A yawn must always be covered with the hand, accompanied by "Excuse me."

- Like the British, respect is given to queues, or lines of people. Never barge or jump into a line; always go politely to the end and wait your turn.

- Finishing a drink, turning the glass upside down, and putting it squarely on the bar is, in some Australian pubs, a signal that you "can whip anyone in the house."

- Sportsmanlike gestures (for example, being a good winner or loser; congratulating a good performance) of any kind are liked and appreciated because good sportsmanship is highly respected.

- Australians are known to be warm, friendly, and informal and dislike overly expressive or "gushy" behavior in any form.

- The more popular and common gestures illustrated and explained in Chapter 2 will probably be known and understood in Australia.

Bangladesh

- Since 85 percent of the population is Muslim, the customary greeting is the *salaam* (see Saudi Arabia).

- Bengalis will shake hands with Western men, but a man merely nods when introduced to a woman of either nationality.

- About 12 percent of the population is Hindu, so among that group the *namaste* is the preferred greeting (hands held chest-high in a prayerlike position).

- Use the right hand for eating—never the left hand. This follows the Middle Eastern custom in which the left hand is used only for bodily hygiene.

- Eating utensils are common in the better restaurants, but it is also acceptable and common to eat with the fingers.

- Men and women often dine separately.

- Visit the washroom, if you must, before and after a meal but not during.

- Among Hindus, it is considered unclean to transfer food from one person's plate to another, even among married couples. Likewise, people will not sip from one another's drinks.

- The thumbs-up gesture is considered an obscene gesture in Bangladesh.

- Remove your shoes before entering a mosque. If you notice other people washing their feet as well, do the same.

- Don't take photographs without asking permission in advance.

- Since Bangladesh is a highly populated country, there might be considerable pushing and shoving in crowds. This is not considered impolite, merely a necessity.

- When an elder enters the room, young people will stand and offer her or him a seat.

China (People's Republic of)

- The Western custom of shaking hands is spreading rapidly and is now probably the customary form of greeting, but often a nod or a slight bow is sufficient. Don't be upset, though, if the Chinese do not smile when being introduced; this is rooted more in the Chinese attitude of keeping feelings inside rather than displaying them openly.

- Guests are usually introduced to the most senior Chinese person present first. If there are many Chinese present, the first few may be introduced in order of rank.

- After introductions and the exchange of business cards, everyone is seated and Chinese tea is usually offered as a refreshment. It's probable the tea will be served in a lidded teacup with tea leaves floating on the water. Blow lightly on the tea or use the teacup lid to brush the leaves aside.

- Business cards are often exchanged, and yours should be printed in your own *and* in the Chinese language. Also, it is more respectful to present your card— or a gift or any other article— using *both* hands.

- Hugging and kissing when greeting are *un*common.

- Generally speaking, the Chinese are not a touch-oriented society.

This is especially true for visitors. So avoid touching or any prolonged form of body contact.

- The younger generation is increasingly engaging in public displays of affection, but among older generations, it is still rare. You may note schoolgirls walking hand-in-hand, and young boys with their arms around each other. These are simply gestures of friendship.

- Avoid being physically demonstrative, especially with older or more senior people.

- Posture is important, so don't slouch or put your feet on desks or chairs. Also, avoid using your feet to gesture or move articles around.

- Personal space is rather limited in China. This means when conversing, the Chinese will stand much closer than Westerners. This often results in Westerners moving backward, with the Chinese following along in something of an unintended pas de deux.

- The Chinese are enthusiastic applauders, so don't be surprised if you are greeted with group clapping, even by small children. When a person is applauded in this fashion it is the custom for that person to return the applause.

- The Chinese suck in air quickly and audibly through the lips and teeth as a reaction to pain, whereas among the Japanese this indicates a negative reaction to something. When something surprising or difficult is proposed or requested, the Chinese may shake their head from left to right without saying a word. When this is done, it would be best to modify your request rather than risk having your Chinese counterpart face the highly embarrassing (for them) situation of having to say "no."

- When walking in public places, direct eye contact and staring are not common in the larger cities, especially in those areas accustomed to foreign visitors. However, in smaller communities, visitors may be the subject of much curiosity and therefore you may notice some stares, especially if you are blond or redheaded.

- Silence can be a virtue in China, so don't be dismayed if there are periods of silence in your dinner or business conversations. It is a sign of politeness and of contemplation. During conversations, be especially careful about interrupting.

- Don't begin eating until the host picks up his or her chopsticks.

- It is the Chinese way to decline gifts or other offerings two or even three times, even when they want to accept, as a matter of etiquette.

- Seating arrangements are important, whether at business meetings or while dining. At meetings, the chief guest is always seated at the "head of the room," facing the door; the host with his or her back to the door. While dining, the primary host sits facing the door and the secondary host sits at the opposite end of the table facing the host. Guests having the highest status sit on either side of the primary host. The remainder of the guests are seated next to the guests of highest status in order of their importance. Guests of lesser importance are seated near the secondary host.

- Before taking any photographs of local people, ask their permission.

- If you wish to smoke, ask permission from those around you. Chinese women rarely smoke, however. If you object to others smoking in your presence, this may pose a difficult situation since segregated smoking areas are uncommon in China. If this is extremely important to you, one gambit is to explain to your host that you are allergic to cigarette smoke.

- The open hand is used for pointing (*not* one finger).

- To beckon someone, the palm faces downward and the fingers are moved in a scratching motion.

- On public streets, spitting and blowing the nose without the benefit of a handkerchief are fairly common, although the government is waging a campaign to reduce this. It is regarded as ridding the body of a waste and is therefore considered an act of personal hygiene.

- Dining revolves around the use of chopsticks. Just watch your host for tips and techniques. Here are some finer points:

  — With wooden chopsticks, you may see the Chinese first rub them together before eating. This is merely a way of removing any possible splinters. But, if you are a guest, it is impolite to do this because it suggests you have been given cheap, rough chopsticks.

  — Even though there will be communal dishes of food, don't take your portions with the ends of the chopsticks you have put in your mouth. Either your host will place food on your plate, or a separate pair of "serving" chopsticks will be near the serving dish.

— Don't stick your chopsticks upright in your rice. Among some superstitious Chinese this could bring bad luck. In some areas placing chopsticks in rice in this fashion is done as an offering to the dead.

— Don't worry if you drop a chopstick on the floor. Some Chinese believe this means you will get an invitation to dinner.

— Don't suck on your chopsticks.

— To eat large pieces of food (when a knife is not available for cutting), it is perfectly acceptable to lift the morsel to your mouth with the chopsticks and bite off a piece.

— When you are finished eating, place your chopsticks in parallel across your dish or bowl.

• The Chinese will hold bowls of food directly under their lower lip and use the chopsticks to push the food into their mouths. When eating long, slippery noodles it is perfectly acceptable to place one end in your mouth and slurp or suck up the remainder.

• Refusing food may be considered impolite. If you don't wish to eat it, just poke it around and move it to the side of your dish.

• Bones are often placed directly on the table alongside your dish.

• Toothpicks are commonly available and used during and after a Chinese meal. Just be certain to cover your mouth with the other hand while poking and picking.

• Offering toasts is common in China and is a relatively simple and uninvolved act: just raise your glass, look at your host and those around him, nod, and drink. You may also say *Kan-pei*, which means "bottoms up," and some Chinese will actually invert the glass "bottom up" to show they have finished the whole drink.

• Don't worry about a bit of pushing and shoving in stores or when groups board public buses or trains. Apologies are neither offered nor expected.

• Most of the more popular gestures discussed in Chapter 2 will be familiar to the Chinese. However, many Chinese will not recognize the "O.K." sign; instead, the thumbs-up signal is known and means "Everything is O.K." When beckoning, the curling inward of the index finger is not used in China.

Fiji

- Fijians greet one another by nodding and bidding each other *"bula,"* or welcome. Otherwise, the handshake is the customary greeting with visitors.

- The custom here is to remove your shoes when entering a home.

- Fijians love to laugh, so you will find much joviality here.

- To exhibit respect when speaking to another person, stand with your arms folded behind your back.

- It is considered impolite to touch a Fijian's head. (Yes, it's true that the impulse to touch a Fijian's head may not be the strongest or most common, but just in case. . . .)

- Beckoning is done by extending the hand, palm downward, and scratching toward you.

- When speaking with someone, direct eye contact is good, but avoid prolonged staring.

- It is impolite to remain standing when you enter a house.

- Never decline gifts or food from a Fijian. This is considered impolite and discourteous.

- It is disrespectful to wear bathing suits in or near a Fijian village unless you are walking along a beach that is classified as a public thoroughfare.

Hong Kong

- After almost a century as a British Crown Colony, many British customs prevail. This includes the straightforward, traditional shaking of hands. If there is any variation, it might be that the grip is less firm than in the United States, and the Chinese may stand closer than Americans or Europeans do.

- When conversing, conspicuous blinking of the eyes is considered impolite. It suggests disrespect and boredom.

- To beckon someone, extend the arm, palm downward, and make a scratching motion with the fingers. Never use the index finger, palm up and toward you, in a back and forth curling motion toward your body. That gesture is used only for animals.

- To signal a waiter that you wish the check or bill, make a writing motion with your two hands.

- The Chinese population here is uncomfortable with any casual or prolonged bodily contact. However, two Chinese of the same sex will be seen on occasion walking along hand-in-hand. This nearly always signifies nothing more than friendship.

- When seated, it is the custom to place the hands in the lap and not wiggle the legs.

- When pointing to something, do so with the open hand and not just one or two fingers.

- When dining, Asian and Western customs are both common and often intermixed. So be prepared for the use of chopsticks as well as knives and forks. With the latter, the Continental style is used, with the fork remaining constantly in the left hand. (See the section on the China [People's Republic of] for more information on the nuances of using chopsticks.)

- Toasting is common, with the host at a large party often visiting each table to present a toast. One appropriate time to make toasts is when the shark's fin soup is served, a delicacy at Chinese meals and often considered the apex of the meal.

- During business meetings, tea may be served. Don't touch yours until the host begins. If he lets the tea sit untouched for a long period, that may be a signal that the meeting is finished.

- Many of the popular gestures illustrated and described in Chapter 2 will be known in Hong Kong, having been imported by a constant stream of Western, and especially British, visitors.

India

- The traditional greeting in India is the *namaste:* the palms of the hands are pressed together in a praying position and held about chest high, then accompanied with a slight bow forward. Westerners can use the *namaste* as a greeting, and such a show of knowledge about Indian customs will be appreciated. The *namaste* is also used when saying good-bye.

- Men customarily do not touch women in either formal or informal situations.

- A Western woman should not initiate a handshake with a man. Most Indian women will shake hands with foreign women but not men.

- Indian businessmen may indulge in warm and even enthusiastic backpatting and slapping. This is merely a sign of cordiality and friendship.

- Carry and be prepared to exchange business cards.

- When walking the streets, try not to stare, especially at the impoverished; that is considered a way to humiliate them.

- Near temples and other holy places, street salespeople will approach you, hand outstretched, as if wanting to shake your hand. That is merely a ruse to allow them to fasten a religious bracelet on the arm and then demand a donation.

- Showing anger is usually the worst way to accomplish almost anything.

- When taking photographs of people, be sure to ask permission first.

- Ask permission before you smoke cigarettes, pipes, or cigars.

- Whistling in public is considered very impolite.

- Here, as in many places in Asia, public displays of affection are neither common nor considered proper, even among married couples.

- If an Indian smiles and jerks his head backward, it could signal "yes." However, in the south of India, if a person moves his head quickly back and forth it signals, "Yes, I understand what you are saying."

- The head is considered a sacred part of the body. Therefore, don't pat youngsters on the head or touch an older person's head.

- Women should cover their heads when entering a sacred building.

- As in the Middle East, where the feet and soles of the shoes are considered the lowest and dirtiest part of the body, the same is true in India. Therefore, try not to touch anyone or point at anyone with your shoes or their soles.

- A unique gesture in India is to grasp one's earlobes. It expresses remorse or honesty, as a servant might do when scolded.

- When you wish to point, use your chin, the full hand, or maybe the thumb, but *not* a single finger. Pointing with a single finger is used only with inferiors. The chin is not used to point to people who are considered superiors. The best way to signal attention toward something or someone is with the full hand.

- Remove shoes before entering a temple or a mosque. Once inside, don't touch paintings or statues.

- The standard way of beckoning another person is with the arm extended, palm down, and with a scratching motion inward with the fingers.

- Beckoning a waiter is done in different ways: locals may snap their fingers and hiss; Westerners should do it the Western way, but don't use the one-curled-finger method.

- Whereas Europeans might wave good-bye by using the hand and arm in an up-and-down motion, this will probably be interpreted in India as signaling "come here."

- When dining, be certain to wash your hands before and after the meal. If utensils are not offered, the fingertips and full hand (right hand only) are used. Transfer food from the communal dish to your plate with a spoon, not with your fingers.

- Hosts will often serve you, and to refuse food could be an insult. If you have objections to any foods, inform your hosts in advance. Use the *namaste* to respectfully signal that you have had enough food.

- The left hand should be used sparingly; pass gifts or other articles with the right hand, eat with the right hand, and point with the right hand.

- A few of the popular gestures described and illustrated in Chapter 2 will be known in India, having been imported over the decades by many visitors. It is wise to use them sparingly, however, and before you do, ask local friends about their local interpretation.

Indonesia

- Indonesia is made up of 17,000 islands and islets, and the nation is made up of 300 ethnic groups. The do's and taboos you find here generally apply to large urban areas. Individual islands also have specific rules of gestures and body language too numerous to mention here.

- When meeting for the first time, congratulating someone, or when saying good-bye, the handshake, accompanied by a slight nod of the head, is the customary gesture for both men and women. In West Java, people greet each other as the Thais do, by placing the palms together, extending the fingertips toward the chin, and nodding the head.

- Never fail to use Mr., Mrs., or Miss when addressing others.

- Men rarely touch women in public except to shake hands.

- Foreign visitors should refrain from kissing in public. This is not only improper but it could even generate anger.

- If you cross your legs when seated, cross them at the knees or the ankles but not with one ankle propped on the other knee.

- If you are seated and your host or hostess enters the room, be sure to rise.

- Indonesians hate to disappoint people, so they will rarely disagree in public and they will smile to mask anger, shock, or embarrassment. It is also impolite to laugh at someone else's mistake or misfortune.

- In tourist areas, street salespeople will crowd closely and even touch you in order to get your attention.

- Indonesians respond to praise with a smile and a nod, but no more. They are uncomfortable with excessive acts of gratitude and also with loud voices and any outward bursts of anger.

- Eating while walking on the street is inappropriate.

- Yawning in public is extremely impolite, but if necessary should be accompanied by covering the mouth.

- Watch your host, but it may be the custom where you are visiting to remove your shoes before entering certain places, like carpeted rooms, feasting places, funerals, and holy places.

- Remove your sunglasses and hat when speaking to someone or entering a home.

- People in Bali may be seen topless and washing and bathing in streams and rivers while in the nude. Do not take photographs.

- Avoid showing the sole of your shoe in the presence of other people.

- Indonesians don't use the left hand very much. Use the right hand for giving or accepting objects and for eating.

- Beckoning someone is done by extending the arm, palm downward, and then making a scratching motion toward your body.

- It is considered impolite to put your hands in your pockets or on your waist while standing and conversing with another person.

- You can pat the shoulder of a close friend to express approval, but not someone older than you or of higher status. Be sure to avoid touching anyone's head.

- Most Indonesians, especially the Javanese, point by extending the thumb or hand instead of the forefinger. Never use your finger to point to another person or to make a point in a meeting.

- Using the head for gestures or to make faces is impolite, as is tossing an object or article to another person.

- Fingers can be used for eating, but utensils are also used. When at the dining table, keep both hands on the table. Avoid using toothpicks in public.

- In crowded restaurants, it is not uncommon for others to ask if they may sit at your table.

- To beckon a waiter, just raise your hand. To call for the bill, make a writing motion with both hands.

- If you are a guest, wait for your host to invite you to begin eating. Then, during the dinner, don't be concerned if the conversation is sparse; Indonesians consider it impolite to talk while eating.

- In some places, when you finish eating, leave just a little food on your plate. If you clean the plate, it is a signal that you would like more food.

- On public buses, it is customary for men to give up their seats to women and for men and women to offer their seats to the elderly.

- Avoid standing with your back to someone, especially to the elderly and high-ranking officials.

Japan

- As most visitors already know, the graceful act of bowing is the traditional greeting for the Japanese. However, the Japanese have also adopted the Western practice of shaking hands, albeit with a light grip and perhaps with eyes averted. The reasons are that a firm grip to them suggests aggression, and direct eye contact is considered slightly intimidating. It should be added, however, that many well-traveled Japanese are carefully studying Western ways and therefore may surprise you with a *firm* grip and *direct* eye contact.

- Meanwhile, to show respect for their customs, it would flatter them to offer a slight bow when being introduced. (For additional comments on the art of bowing, see pages 21–25).

- Displays of emotion— fear, anger, exuberance—are rare among the Japanese because they are taught to suppress any such displays, especially in public.

- Scratching the head is one signal that a Japanese is trying to hide confusion or embarrassment.

- In Japan, when walking directly in front of someone, as in a theater or crowded room, the polite gesture is to hold out your hand with the edge downward as if you are cutting your way through.

- Standing with arms folded across the chest signals that a Japanese person is thinking intently.

- Unlike the Western world, where it is considered rude to make noises when eating soup or noodles, among the Japanese it is perfectly acceptable to make audible "slurping" sounds.

- Even the smallest gesture may have meaning in Japan, so it is important to refrain from expansive arm and hand movements, exaggerated facial expressions, or dramatic gestures of any kind.

- Women should avoid wearing high heels so as not to risk towering over Japanese counterparts.

- The seemingly simple act of exchanging business cards is more complex in Japan because the business card represents not only one's identity but one's station in life. Here are some tips on what you may encounter:

  — The business card is held with both hands, grasped between the thumbs and forefingers.

  — It is extended forward in a respectful gesture with the printing pointed considerately toward the other person. A slight bow is made at the same time.

  — The Japanese will take the card, again with both hands and a reciprocal bow, and then read the card carefully. This may be followed by another slight bow.

  — After this sequence, the Western handshake may occur. (Or, in deference to the Westerner, the greeting may begin with handshaking and then evolve to bowing and the ritual of exchanging business cards.)

— When Westerners take the business card from a Japanese, they should avoid examining it casually and quickly tucking it into a coat or shirt pocket. Examine it carefully, then place it on the table in front of you for further reference.

— Avoid scribbling notes on the back of the card. This shows a certain measure of disrespect for something that represents a person's identity.

• Avoid clapping a Japanese on the back, standing very close, any form of public kissing, or any prolonged physical contact. On crowded public transportation, however, it is a different matter. People are accustomed to being jammed into tight spaces, as epitomized by the transit employees whose jobs consist of packing people into the public trains before the doors close.

• When in meetings, periods of silence may occur. This is perfectly acceptable and customary. During these periods, the Japanese may even raise their eyes to look over the heads of others while contemplating.

• Queues are generally respected; it is only in crowded train and subway stations where the huge volume of people causes touching and pushing.

• Because of the high regard for graciousness and restraint, one should not shout, raise the voice in anger, or exhibit any excessively demonstrative behavior.

• Among the Japanese, smiling often can cover a gamut of emotions: happiness, anger, confusion, apologies, or sadness.

• Displaying an open mouth is considered rude in Japan. That is one reason many Japanese, especially the women, cover their mouths when giggling or laughing.

• The Japanese have great difficulty voicing an outright "no" to a question or statement. In fact, as they listen to you speaking, they may nod their head as if agreeing or indicating "yes." But do not take this as agreement. Waving the hand back and forth in front of one's own face (palm outward) is one way of saying "I don't know" or "I don't understand"—but it is also done in the context of humility, as when receiving a compliment, signaling "No, I am undeserving."

- Correct posture is important in Japan, especially when seated. Consequently, avoid slouching or putting your feet on a table or stool. Balance in life is a basic Japanese principle, so a square, solid posture when seated or walking is practiced (for example, both feet squarely on the ground, arms in the lap or on the armrests). Any slouching or leaning back in a tipped chair can be interpreted as showing an "I don't care" attitude.

- Listening is considered not only polite in Japan but also is regarded as a valuable business skill. Americans and other Westerners tend to interrupt. In fact, author John C. Condon writes that the three top complaints the Japanese have about Americans are that they talk too much, they interrupt, and they don't listen.

- Crossing the legs at the knees or ankles is the preferred form rather than with one ankle over the other knee.

- To get the attention of a waiter, catch his eye and dip your head downward.

- To beckon someone, put your arm out, palm down, and make a scratching motion with the fingers.

- It is considered insulting to point to someone with four fingers extended and the thumb folded into the palm.

- When the hand and fingers are used to count, the Japanese use the thumb to represent the number "five." Therefore the thumbs-up gesture in Japan can signify the number "five."

- The "O.K." gesture in Japan may be interpreted as the signal for "money," probably because the circular shape formed by the index finger and thumb suggests the shape of a coin. For example, a Japanese may make a purchase at a food counter and then flash this gesture to signal "Give me my change in coins."

- When a Japanese is speaking in his own language, he may gesture with one hand, fingers slightly pursed, and point the hand slightly at himself—toward his face. This is simply an emphatic way of saying "I" or "me" or "myself."

- In many restaurants, it is the custom for men to sit cross-legged on the floor. Women should sit either on their legs or have them tucked to one side. For Westerners who find this uncomfortable, Japanese restaurants often provide a small armrest, allowing you to sit with legs folded on one side while leaning your weight on the armrest.

- Bathing in Japanese baths is a new experience for most visitors because it is usually done in stages. It can involve soaking in one tub, exiting to soap and lather up, rinsing, and then entering a new tub. Avoid soaping up, rinsing, and soaking all in one tub.

- Blowing your nose in public is considered rude. In Japan, the handkerchief is used primarily for wiping the mouth or drying the hands when leaving the washroom. Paper tissues are used for blowing the nose and then discarded. Chewing gum in business meetings is also considered impolite.

- Many Japanese will be seen in public wearing white gauze masks, like those used in a hospital surgery room. This is not because they fear air pollution, but instead because they probably have a cold and do not wish to pass along the germs to others.

- Present a gift with both hands, as with business cards. This is viewed as a gesture of humility, and humility is important in Japan. It is a nice touch to bow slightly while doing either act. Also, when receiving a gift, you are not expected to open it right then and there. Wait until later, in private.

- Avoid standing with your hand or hands in your pockets, especially when greeting someone or when addressing a group of people.

- If you are eating with chopsticks, follow some of the customs outlined in the earlier section on China (see page 177). However, the Japanese hold bowls of food lower and not right under the chin.

- When eating, pick up dishes on your left side with your right hand and vice versa.

- Toasting is quite common in Japan. It is a simple action of raising the glass and saying one word, *Kan-pei,* which literally means "Drain the cup," or as Westerners might say, "Bottoms up."

- At public restaurants or private homes, it is often the custom to remove your shoes before entering. You'll either see a lineup of other shoes from other restaurant patrons at the doorstep, or just follow the actions of your host. Shoes are usually placed with the toes pointing toward the exit.

- A formal Japanese tea ceremony is just that—a ceremony. It is grace-ful, expressive, and artistic. Watch your host for the proper proce-dure.

- In summary, for most visitors the Japanese customs are complex and difficult to understand. Remember two things: (1) style, or the *way* things are done, is just as important as substance, or *what* is being done; and (2) watch your Japanese hosts carefully and follow their example.

Korea, South

- Among themselves, bowing is the traditional form for both greeting and departing. Western and Korean male friends usually greet with both a slight bow and shaking hands. When shaking hands, both hands are sometimes used to express special affection or sympathy. Women usually do not extend their hands, especially toward men, but usually just nod slightly.

- The senior person offers to shake hands first, but the junior person bows first.

- Business cards are traded respectfully. Read the card carefully and save it. Keep the card on the table in front of you as just one small ges-ture of respect.

- Friends may make eye contact, but it is considered disrespectful for a younger person or someone in a junior position to make eye contact with an older or more senior person. This often indicates defiance.

- Two men or two women may be seen walking along holding hands, and it is merely a sign of friendship, nothing more. But in almost all other situations, avoid touching, gripping, or patting a Korean on the arm, shoulder, or back unless you are *very* good friends.

- In public situations, however, personal space is very limited and Western visitors may be disconcerted by the closeness of others in markets, on buses, or while walking on the sidewalks.

- When saying good-bye, the traditional gesture is the bow, but the younger generation has adopted the Western custom of waving good-bye by moving the arm side to side. Do not hold your arm out in front of you and move your fingers up and down. This means "come here," not "good-bye."

- The Western version of gesturing "come here"—arm and hand up, palm toward the face—is used only for calling dogs. The correct way to beckon someone in Korea is to extend the arm, palm down, and make a scratching motion.

- When you are standing and having a conversation with someone, a Korean may pass between the two of you instead of walking around. The polite thing is to step backward to allow the person through. The reason for this is that in Korea it is impolite to make someone walk behind your back.

- When walking in public, the convention in Korea is to keep to the left side of the walkway.

- Avoid putting your foot or feet up on a table or chair, or slouching when seated.

- Koreans, especially women, will cover their mouths when laughing. This is because it is considered impolite to show the inside of your mouth.

- Shoes are removed before entering a Korean home.

- Koreans, like other Asians, like to avoid saying "no," but one gesture that is often used by men to signal "no" or that "something is very difficult" is to tip the head backward and audibly suck air in through the teeth.

- Loud talking or laughing is usually avoided, unless the occasion is business entertainment. Then, after dinner, there may be solo and group singing and much laughter.

- Older people receive much respect in Korea, so it is appropriate to rise when a person—especially an elderly man—enters the room.

- Laughter is used to disguise many emotions: anger, frustration, and even fear.

- Avoid eating food while walking along a public street.

- When dining, chopsticks will probably be used. Follow the same general instructions given earlier in the section on China. (See page 177.)

- When dining, the elderly are served first and the children last.

- During a dinner, a small communal cup of wine or liquor may be passed along; drink from it and pass it back to the person who gave it to you. It is also polite for you to fill your neighbor's small soy sauce dish and vice versa.

- Avoid pouring your own drink. It is usually done for you, and you should offer to pour for others. Lift up your glass when receiving a drink, and when you pour for others support your forearm with the other hand. (If all this sounds a bit complicated, just watch how the Koreans around you do it.)

- Drunkenness is quickly forgiven in Korea unless it is accompanied by either gross or aggressive behavior.

- After a Korean dinner, if there is group or solo singing, try to go along with the fun. If asked to sing solo, the polite response is to sing—no matter how simple the song or how poorly you sing.

- At a restaurant, one person usually pays for all, and there may be good-natured argument over the right to pay. Usually, the elder person pays for the younger.

- Blowing the nose in public is considered rude. Also, dispose of tissues rather than returning them to a pocket or purse.

- Don't open a gift the moment it is received; instead, wait until later, in private.

- Food and other objects are passed using the right hand, often with the left hand supporting the right forearm.

- As in other Asian countries, proper posture is important. Stand or sit erectly or squarely. Do not cross your legs in public, especially in front of someone who is older or senior in position to you. Try to keep your hands in sight of the person you are talking with.

- If you are wearing sunglasses, remove them during any conversation with another person.

- Toothpicks may be offered at the end of a meal and it is acceptable to use them in front of others, but be certain to cover your mouth with the other hand.

- Periods of silence are common and accepted, especially during dinners. Don't be disturbed if there are gaps in the conversation.

- It is considered impolite to enter a room without knocking first. However, Koreans may not wait for you to come to the door and open it. They may knock and then enter. This also applies in public toilets where locks may not function. In these cases, if you are occupying a public toilet stall, just clear your throat or knock back to signal that your stall is in use.

- Bathroom doors are usually kept closed, so knock or make a slight cough first to determine if the bathroom is in use.

- When you enter a conference or dining room, wait to be directed to the seat designated for you. Even if you are the guest of honor, do not proceed directly to the chair of honor. In fact, you may even make slight protestations about accepting the highest seat. This demonstrates humility and is appreciated by Koreans.

- Many of the gestures described and illustrated in Chapter 2 will be known in Korea, mainly because they have been imported by Westerners. But use them with caution, and if at all possible ask Korean friends about them.

Malaysia

- There are three distinct cultures here: Malay (53 percent), Chinese (32 percent), and Indian (11 percent)—each with its own customs. Various indigenous groups account for the balance. Among the main three, shaking hands is the customary greeting, but watch for these differences:

  — Chinese of different sexes will shake hands, but not the Malays or Indians, and if a Chinese woman wishes to shake hands she will make the first move. Chinese men will also often greet one another with a friendly pat on the arm. The Chinese are uncomfortable with any hugging or kissing, unless you are unusually good friends.

  — Malays will often bow slightly when greeting others. This may be accompanied by the *salaam* gesture of greeting: offering one or both hands and lightly touching the hands of the other person, then bringing the hand(s) to the heart, signifying, "I greet you from my heart." Both hands are used when greeting older or more senior people as a sign of respect.

  — Indians may greet you with the *namaste*, placing the hands in a prayerlike position, chest high, and bowing slightly.

- The Chinese are extremely hospitable and will never reveal if you have committed an error in behavior. So, watch for little signals—a quizzical expression, an upturned eye—and then subtly inquire of a friend if you have inadvertently erred.

- Give respect to elderly people: open doors for them, give up your seat to them, and don't smoke without asking their permission first.

- Smiling or laughing at someone else's discomfort or misfortune is used to cover up embarrassment.

- Among the Malays and Indians, avoid touching someone else's head. That is where they believe the spirit or soul resides. In fact, people of the opposite sex should avoid any kind of casual touching of one another.

- Since showing the sole of the shoe is considered rude, try to keep your feet planted firmly on the ground. Also, don't use your feet for pointing or for moving objects.

- When a person stands with hands on hips, it is a sign of anger.

- Smacking your closed fist into the palm of the other hand is considered a rude gesture.

- Among the Malays, avoid pointing with your forefinger. Instead, point with the thumb, with the other four fingers curled into the palm.

- To beckon someone, never use the index finger in a curling motion. Instead, extend the arm, palm down, and make a scratching motion toward you with your fingers.

- Always cover your mouth when yawning.

- Among the Malays and Indians, the rule while dining is to use only the right hand. The left hand is used for bodily hygiene and is therefore considered unclean and should not be used for touching others or passing along gifts or other objects.

- Remove your shoes before entering mosques and Malay homes.

- In homes and certain public buildings, if you are seated on the floor, men sit cross-legged while women customarily sit with their legs tucked under them.

- To get a waiter's attention, just raise your hand. Avoid hissing, shouting, or pointing with one finger.

- At the dinner table, it is considered rude to blow your nose or clear your throat in front of others. Go to the washroom and do these actions in private.

- Malays eat with their right hand only and spoons. You may use a fork in the left hand to push food into the spoon that is held in the right hand.

- Indians eat with the fingers of the right hand, while guests will usually be provided with a fork and spoon. Indians never soil the fingers above the first knuckle and never suck or lick the fingers to clean them.

- The Chinese eat with chopsticks and spoons—the spoons are used for soups and other liquid foods. Using the left hand to eat is perfectly acceptable among the Chinese.

- Some superstitions among the Chinese while eating: placing your chopsticks across your plate signals that you are still hungry, instead, place them on the little "resting stand"; never stick a chopstick upright in a bowl of rice because this is a symbol used at a Chinese funeral; waving chopsticks in the air to gesture is bad manners; slurping soup and belching during a meal are both acceptable. (See pages 179–80 for additional guidelines for eating with chopsticks.)

- Among the Malays, when toasting or handing a dish to another person, it shows respect if you do as follows: use the right hand, but allow the left hand to support the right at the wrist or forearm.

- Malayans queue, or form a line, for public buses. Often during rush hour in the cities, however, you may see Malaysians jumping the queues.

- If you see a prayer rug in a Muslim's office or home, be certain not to stand on it or touch it with your feet.

- Indians have a unique way of indicating agreement: they move their head quickly from side to side. Many Westerners misread this gesture as meaning "no."

- Indians never use the left hand for social purposes—ever!

- As a final note, because of these mixed cultures and the slight differences between them, the best guideline is to observe your host and others around you and follow their example.

Myanmar (formerly Burma)

- It is *not* customary to shake hands, but many businesspeople may adopt the Western custom of handshaking, so be prepared either way.

- It is not proper to show physical expressions of affection in public.

- Buddhism is widely practiced here, and in that religion the bottom half of the body is considered lowly. The upper half of the body is regarded with greater esteem.

- The head of the image of Buddha should not be touched.

- The feet are considered unclean, and therefore it is very rude to raise your feet, such as placing them on a table or desktop.

- You may note that people remove their shoes before entering a home, and always before entering any religious building.

New Zealand

- The conventional handshake with firm grip and direct eye contact is the custom here.

- The original inhabitants were the Polynesian Maori and, while they are a minority now, their culture still thrives. The traditional greeting among Maori tribespeople is to press noses.

- The large majority of the population is of British descent, therefore, many British customs for body language and gestures prevail.

- Loud speech and excessive demonstrative behavior are frowned upon.

- Chewing gum and using toothpicks in public are considered bad manners.

- New Zealanders eat in the Continental style, meaning fork constantly in the left hand, knife in the right.

- Be sure to cover the mouth when yawning.

- Ask permission before photographing anyone, especially the Maori.

- Most of the more popular gestures described in Chapter 2 will be known in New Zealand with special attention to the "V" for Victory sign—as in England, if done with the palm *inward* it is a very rude gesture.

Okinawa

- The traditional greeting here is the bow, both when meeting and when departing. However, because of the strong and long Western influence, handshaking is also common.

- Many of the practices concerning closeness, touching, and open displays of affection that are found in Japan are also prevalent here.

- When entering a private home, it is usually customary to remove your shoes and place them with the toes pointing toward the outdoors.

- The following body actions are important:

  — Avoid yawning in public situations.

  — Posture is important, so don't slouch when sitting and try to maintain a balanced posture at all times.

  — If you cross your legs, do so at the knees and not with one ankle on top of the other knee.

  — Laughter not only signals pleasure but is also used to mask embarrassment.

  — Avoid eating on the street.

- Chopsticks are used when dining, although Western utensils are freely available. (See the section on China, page 177, for complete guidelines on proper use of chopsticks.)

Pakistan

- The handshake is the common greeting, although with a more gentle grip than Westerners may use. Close friends of the same sex may embrace. A Western man should refrain from touching or shaking hands with a Pakistani woman unless she offers her hand. Western women, however, may extend a hand to be shaken by a Pakistani man.

- It is the custom to be greeted with an offer of coffee, tea, or other refreshment. The custom is always to accept, otherwise you may risk offending your host.

- Since this is a Muslim country, many of the gestures and body language found in the Middle East will apply here. These include such things as:

  — Eat only with the right hand because the left hand is used for bodily hygiene and is considered unclean.

  — Women are often kept separated in social situations.

  — Women dress and act modestly in all settings.

  — Two men may be seen walking along holding hands. This is nothing more than a sign of friendship.

  — The Muslim practice of praying five times each day is strictly observed here, so don't object or interrupt if someone is praying.

  — Avoid trying to photograph Pakistani women, at least without asking permission beforehand.

  — The sole of the shoe is considered lowly and dirty, so avoid pointing or showing it to another person.

- In public settings, Pakistani men may be what Western women would consider forward. Occasional bumping or touching may occur; Western women should avoid any actions such as casual physical or eye contact that could be interpreted as encouragement.

- Staring is common in the Pakistani culture. Don't be offended if you find yourself the object of a steady gaze.

- One obscene gesture in Pakistani is the *closed fist*.

- Remove your shoes before entering a mosque. Avoid walking in front of someone who is praying. Speak in whispers. Don't touch any objects, and don't smoke.

- Dining is done with Western utensils. Use the fork in the left hand to push food into the spoon, held in the right hand.

- Public buses are notoriously crowded, with much touching, pushing, and shoving.

Philippines

- Handshaking is the common custom, with both men and women shaking hands in a friendly and informal fashion. With children, it is best to let them initiate the greeting as a sign that they know how to be respectful. A Filipino child may even take a visitor's hand and press it against his own forehead as a gesture of respect.

- Filipinos may greet one another with the "eyebrow flash" which is merely a quick lifting of the eyebrows.

- Two women may be seen holding hands in public, but this usually represents nothing more than friendship. Men do not hold hands in public.

- Staring at someone is considered rude.

- Respect is always shown to elderly people.

- Speaking in a loud voice is considered ill-mannered and rude.

- As in other parts of the Far East, laughter is used to convey both enjoyment and pleasure but also to mask embarrassment over another person's misfortune.

- Overimbibing alcohol is considered rude, and being rude is generally a strong taboo in Southeast Asia, particularly in Indonesia, Thailand, and the Philippines.

- Before taking photographs, always request the permission of your subjects.

- Filipino women rarely, if ever, smoke in public.

- Instead of pointing to an object, Filipinos will shift their eyes toward it, or purse the lips and point with the mouth.

- If you stand with your hands on your hips, it will be interpreted by Filipinos as a sign that you are angry or challenging another person.

- To beckon someone, never curl your index finger back and forth because that is considered insulting. The proper way to beckon is to extend the arm, palm down, and move the fingers in a scratching motion. The best way to call a waiter is to simply raise the hand, with fingers held closely together.

- Dining is done with Western utensils, but the fork is often held in the left hand and used to push food into the spoon, which is held in the right hand.

- Try to leave a bit of food on your plate to signal to your host that he or she has provided enough food.

- During business entertaining, as in South Korea, you may be asked to participate in single or group singing. Try to go along with the fun.

- When using public transportation, Filipinos queue or observe orderly lines.

- Because of the long American presence in these islands, Filipinos will recognize most of the popular gestures shown in Chapter 2.

Samoa

- Greetings are usually rather formal and flowery in speech. Samoans enjoy eloquent speech. Visitors are encouraged to reply in kind. Foreign visitors to Samoa are not expected to be familiar with Samoa oratory, but polite greeting are appreciated.

- When visiting a Samoan home, don't enter until the mats have been spread on the floor. Then leave your shoes at the door. When seated on these mats, sit cross-legged.

- Conversation is conducted while seated.

- Avoid stretching your legs out in front of you because pointing your feet at your host or toward the middle of the home is impolite. If you must stretch your legs, cover them with a mat.

- Don't eat while standing inside a home, or while walking in the roads and streets.

- The national beverage is *kava;* when it is offered to you it is customary to spill a few drops before drinking.

Singapore

- Because of the strong and long British influence, the Island of Singapore follows many British traditions. Therefore, a handshake is the conventional form of greeting, and if the person is Asian it might be accompanied with a slight bow. When introduced to a woman, it is best to let her make the first move toward handshaking.

- Bear in mind, however, that Singapore's population is made up of several ethnic groups, which have their own customs. These groups include Chinese, Muslims, and Indians.

- The elderly receive great respect: hold doors for them, rise when they enter the room, and give up your seat for them on public transportation.

- Some improprieties among non-British ethnic groups:

    — Don't touch someone on top of the head; among many non-British residents, it is believed this is where the spirit resides.

    — When crossing the legs, do so at the knees so that the sole of your shoe is not displayed to other people.

    — Since the foot is considered the lowliest and dirtiest part of the body, do not use your feet to touch or move other objects.

    — Avoid beckoning someone by curling the index finger back and forth. The proper way to beckon someone is to extend the arm, palm down, and wiggle the fingers in a scratching motion.

- Littering in public is absolutely forbidden, and if a person is caught, he or she can be subjected to heavy fines. This even includes discarded cigarettes.

- Keep in mind that Singapore's residents include many Malaysians (Malays, Chinese, Indians), so be certain to be familiar with the list of gestures for Malaysia as well.

Sri Lanka

- The culture here is strongly influenced by British traditions, so handshaking British-style will be common. However, there are also many different ethnic groups and castes and each of these will have its own nuances when people greet one another.

- Aside from the handshake, the other traditional greeting is called the *ayubowan* and is similar to the *namaste.* Westerners are not expected to initiate this form of greeting, but it would show politeness and respect to perform this in return.

- Sri Lankan women will be comfortable shaking hands with any Westerner. Western men should, however, avoid embracing Sri Lankan women when greeting.

- Extinguish a cigarette before meeting someone.

- Sri Lankans often smile instead of saying "thank you." However, Western women should be cautious about smiling too much in public. A smile is also considered a form of flirtation.

- A caste system still exists here, so if you invite someone to sit down and he or she is reluctant, don't keep insisting.

- Nodding the head up and down signifies agreement or understanding, while shaking it back and forth indicates "no." This is the same as the Western custom.

- As in many Middle Eastern and Asian countries, the left hand is used for bodily hygiene and so is considered the unclean hand. Therefore, eat only with your right hand, and when passing objects from one person to another, use only your right hand.

- Remove shoes and hat when entering a mosque or temple.

- Any image of Buddha is considered sacred, so don't touch one and *never* lean or sit on one.

Tahiti

- Shake hands when introduced in Tahiti. In fact, it is the custom to carefully shake hands with everyone present. If you don't, it is considered impolite. Because of the strong French influence throughout these islands, Tahitian friends will often greet one another by kissing cheeks.

- Remove your shoes before entering a Tahitian home.

- Wash your hands before eating because Tahitians usually eat with their hands.

Taiwan (Republic of China)

- Taiwanese are very accustomed to Western visitors, so the handshake has become a common and accepted greeting. However, a nod of the head with eyes downcast is also sufficient.

- Business cards should be exchanged, and take the time to read the other person's card carefully; place it near you for reference rather than quickly putting it aside or in your pocket.

- Remove shoes before entering a home.

- Great respect is afforded the elderly, so it is important to let your actions reflect this. Speak to them first. Hold doors open for them. Rise when they enter a room. Give up your seat if no others are available. Remove your hat when addressing them.

- One gesture of special respect for the elderly is to cover your left fist with your right hand, raise both hands to your breast, and bow your head with eyes downcast.

- Loud, boisterous, or rude behavior is a strong taboo in Taiwan.

- Youthful friends of the same sex may be seen holding hands, but avoid putting your arm around the shoulders of any Taiwanese.

- A balanced posture is considered important, so Taiwanese men will usually sit with both feet firmly fixed to the floor. Women may cross their legs at the knees or ankles.

- Don't use your feet to move or touch other objects because the feet are considered lowly and dirty. Don't place your feet up on a desk or table.

- The gesture to indicate "no" is to lift your hand to face level, palm facing outward, and move it back and forth like a windshield wiper.

- To point, don't use the index finger; use the whole hand instead.

- To beckon someone, extend the arm, palm downward, and make a scratching motion with the fingers. Never beckon someone using the forefinger in a curling motion, back and forth.

- When dining, chopsticks are the normal utensils, although in restaurants that cater to Westerners, knives and forks, will be available. For tips and guidelines on using chopsticks, refer to the section on China (page 177).

- Toasting, both before and during dinner, is common in Taiwan. The toasting word is *Kan-pei,* which means "bottoms up."

- Always present and receive gifts with *both* hands. It's customary not to open or look at gifts in the presence of the gift-giver. Ask first if in doubt.

- Don't stick your chopsticks straight up in your rice. That looks like sticks of incense burning in the pots in temples and can be seen as a bad omen or simply as being disrespectful to others.

Thailand

- The traditional greeting in Thailand is called the *wai,* where the hands are placed together in a prayerlike position and the head is nodded in a slight bow. It is almost identical to the *namaste* of India. This signifies "hello," "thank you," "good-bye," or even "I'm sorry." When performing the *wai,* the higher the hands the more respect you are conveying, but do not raise the fingertips higher than the face.

- The custom is to remove shoes before entering a home, but some Thais will insist that Westerners keep them on in deference to Western tradition.

- Avoid stepping on doorsills when entering a dwelling. Thais believe a deity resides in the doorsill and stepping there will offend that deity.

- Guests are almost always offered a cold or hot drink and the polite gesture is to accept.

- When dining, a spoon and fork are used—the fork for pushing food into the spoon.

- The most sacred part of the human body is the head. Consequently, avoid touching the top of any person's head. This is often difficult for Westerners who seem to unconsciously pat the heads of young children.

- Conversely, the lowliest parts of the body are the feet, and therefore you should not point your toe or heel or any part of the foot at any person or object. Don't use your feet to move objects, and try to avoid showing the sole of your shoe to anyone because that is regarded as impolite. Never step over another person kneeling or lying on the ground.

- Two Western customs—placing your arm over the back of a chair in which another person is sitting, and affectionately patting someone else's shoulders or back—are both considered improper, even offensive.

- Two Thai men may be seen walking along the street and holding hands. This is merely a sign of friendship. Other gestures of affection are rarely displayed in public places.

- As in many countries in Asia, the smile is used not only to express pleasure and amusement but also to cover up embarrassments of any kind.

- Avoid loud talk, excessive and demonstrative gestures, or any form of anger or boisterous behavior. Do not hug Thais to show appreciation.

- While it may happen only rarely, resist any inclination to throw an object to another person. This is considered rude and impolite in Thailand.

- Pointing with one finger is considered rude and is only done when pointing to objects or animals, never humans. Use your chin or incline your head instead.

- To beckon someone, extend the arm, palm down, and make a scratching motion with the fingers. Don't snap your fingers, hiss, or holler.

- Since the left hand is regarded as unclean, don't eat with it. It is polite to pass objects to another person using both hands.

- It is impolite to stand and converse with someone while placing one or both hands in your pockets.

- Remove your shoes before entering a mosque or a Buddhist temple, and give the greatest respect to images of Buddha and pictures of the king.

- Showing anger is one of the worst things you can do during business negotiations.

- When passing in front of someone, especially a more senior or elderly person, lower the upper body slightly.

CENTRAL AND SOUTH AMERICA

Argentina

- A warm handshake is the custom here. As men become well acquainted, the handshake might be accompanied by a light touch on the forearm or elbow. Good friends will greet with an *abrazo*, or embrace. This may also include several hearty pats on the back.

- Women friends kiss each other on the cheek and shake hands with both hands, but will not usually talk to strangers without first being properly introduced.

- Men and women who are longtime acquaintances may also exchange a light hug and a "pretended kiss" on the cheek. This means merely brushing cheeks together and making a soft sound as if kissing.

- Women friends may be seen walking along the street arm-in-arm.

- When conversing, Argentines may stand closer than North Americans or Europeans do. Also, an Argentine man may touch the arm or shoulder, or even finger the lapel of the man he is speaking with.

- Good eye contact is important. Avoid using overly demonstrative gestures.

- Men usually cross their legs knee-over-knee, but this may be considered unladylike for women.

- Gestures to avoid in Argentina:

  — Standing with the hands on the hips suggests anger, or a challenge.

  — Yawning in public is rude.

  — Slapping the inside of the thighs near the groin is considered an obscene male gesture.

— Never pour wine by grasping the neck of the bottle with the hand and rotating the hand backward so that the palm turns upward. Also, always pour with the right hand, never the left.

• Argentines have strong national pride in their excellent red wines; if and when toasts are made, the proper gesture is simply to raise your glass to those around you and say *"salud"* (which means "health"), then sip.

• To beckon someone, extend the arm, palm down, and make a scratching motion with the fingers.

• Since there is a strong Italian heritage in Argentina, many gestures from that country are known and used. For example:

— Brushing the backs of the fingers under the chin and then outward means "I don't know," or "I don't care."

— The "hook 'em horns" gesture can be interpreted as "Your spouse is cheating on you."

• To signal across a distance to another person that "You have a phone call," Argentines will often point the index finger toward the side of the head and make a circular motion. This can be confusing, because in North America and other regions that gesture can also mean "You are crazy."

• To indicate that something is just "so-so," Argentines will extend the hand and fingers and waggle the thumb up and down: thumb up, then thumb down, repeating it several times.

• Since one of Argentina's most popular sports is soccer, a popular gesture conveying exuberance and victory is to raise the fist upward emphatically, with the knuckles of the fingers pointing outward.

• When dining, many Argentines will cut their meat by placing the fork upright in the meat and putting the knife through the tines for easier cutting.

• To indicate you have finished eating, cross the knife and fork (tines down) in the middle of your plate.

• Some of the popular gestures depicted in Chapter 2 have been imported into Argentina, so they will be known and recognized there. One of those gestures—the "O.K." sign—is a *rude* gesture in the neighboring country of Brazil, so most Argentines will be aware of that gesture and that meaning.

Bolivia

- A warm handshake is the customary greeting. Good male friends will also perform an *abrazo*, or embrace, accompanied by a few hearty pats on the back, and then maybe even another handshake. Female friends will also embrace and touch cheeks in a kissing motion.

- If a person believes his hand is dirty or soiled in any way, he may offer his forearm to shake.

- When two men are standing and conversing, North Americans and Europeans may find themselves feeling uncomfortable because Bolivians (and most Latin Americans) seem to stand so close. There is no hidden symbolism or message here, it's merely that personal space is less or narrower.

- When conversing, good eye contact is important. Not to do so is considered impolite.

- The "fig" gesture, hand forming a fist with the thumb protruding between index and middle finger, is considered a rude gesture in Bolivia.

- In a marketplace, if a vendor holds his hand out, fingers extended, and flips the thumb back and forth, it merely means "There isn't any left; I don't have any more."

- When yawning, always cover the mouth.

- To beckon someone, extend the arm, palm downward, and move the fingers in a scratching motion.

- When dining, never eat with the fingers. This even pertains to eating chicken. A special fork is often provided for eating fruit.

- At the dinner table, don't put your hands in your lap. Keep them above the table, perhaps resting the wrists lightly on the edge of the table.

- When pouring wine, it is considered extremely rude to pour it with the left hand or "backhanded"—that is, turning the hand over so that the palm faces upward.

Brazil

• A good, warm handshake is the traditional greeting in Brazil. However, because the Brazilians show affection easily, among male friends the *abraço* (Portuguese spelling), or embrace, will be added.

• Women friends will add a light kiss on the cheek, with married women kissing both cheeks. If one or both women is single, a third kiss is added signifying a wish for marriage for the single person(s).

• If a Brazilian woman believes she knows a man well enough, during the initial handshake she will draw the man gently forward and offer her cheek to be kissed. Bear in mind this is a "pretended" kiss, with the cheeks just brushing plus a kissing motion.

• People in Brazil will also shake hands when arriving and departing. There may also be a touching of the forearm or elbow, and often a pat on the back.

• Most touching, as well as sustained eye contact (a sign of courtesy), occurs between peers. A younger person would not touch an older person informally, and strangers do not touch. Similarly, there is little eye contact between people of different ages or status. Usually the younger or less powerful person looks down and away. Many Americans mistakenly interpret this indirect eye contact as evasiveness or deceit.

• Don't be alarmed if you see two young women twirling their fingers around each other's hair, or pulling at each other's jewelry, shirt collars, or buttons. There is merely a sign of friendship and a way to stay engaged in conversation. Young women also walk arm-in-arm or hand-in-hand.

• If you are conducting business, be certain to bring a plentiful supply of business cards because these are always exchanged. Also, during business meetings expect to be served (often) small cups of very strong coffee.

• Since this is more of a touching society, people stand close together when conversing or when standing in lines.

• If you see an acquaintance at a distance, it is fine to wave but avoid shouting a greeting.

• Don't eat or chew gum while walking on the street.

- Brazilians use hand and body gestures often, and therefore they have a variety of unique motions and meanings. Here are some of the more important ones to remember:

  — The "O.K." sign, with thumb and forefinger forming a circle, is a rude gesture, especially when the other three fingers protrude outward, away from the body. This refers to a part of the female anatomy and is therefore considered a vulgar gesture.

  — If a Brazilian man wishes to signal that he sees a pretty girl, he will cup both hands together to form a tube, or an imaginary telescope, and look through it at the girl with his eye.

  — To add emphasis to a statement, a Brazilian may snap the fingers while whipping the hand down and out.

  — If you see a Brazilian brush the back of his fingers under his chin and outward, he is indicating "I don't know."

  — To express appreciation, a Brazilian may appear to pinch his ear-lobe between thumb and forefinger. For example, if you've enjoyed a meal, this gesture may be used. Among Brazilians, to dramatize it even further, they will reach behind the head and grasp the opposite earlobe.

  — Whipping the hand and fingers downward with the thumb and forefinger hitting each other is a way of signaling "That is a lot of money."

- The "fig," or *figa* as it is called in Brazil, with the hand forming a fist and with the thumb protruding upward between forefinger and middle finger, is a symbol of *good luck* in Brazil. This is especially important to note because in some Mediterranean countries and even in certain other Latin countries, this is a rude, obscene gesture, regarded as a phallic symbol. But in Brazil, it is possible to buy replicas of this gesture in the form of charms or amulets because of its "good luck" symbolism.

- Punching the fist into a cupped hand is a vulgar gesture.

- When dining, avoid using the fingers to pick up any food unless you wrap it in a napkin. This is done for sanitary reasons and includes sandwiches and fruit.

- Never cut food with the side of your fork—always use a knife.

- When using toothpicks, always cover your mouth with a hand or napkin.

- Don't smoke during a meal. Brazilians customarily wait until the meal is finished.

- Again, for sanitary reasons, don't drink directly from a can or bottle. Even at roadside stops, glasses are usually furnished.

- If and when a toast is offered, it is sufficient simply to lift your glass, say "*saude*," and sip the wine.

- Driving a car in Brazil is a rare—and very risky—experience. Rules of the road respected in many other countries are often good-naturedly disregarded in Brazil.

- When carrying any article along the streets—a pair of shoes, a bottle, a box of candy—it is customary to have it wrapped in a bag or some paper.

- As indicated, you will find Brazil a montage of gestures, so be aware and be certain to ask for interpretations if you spot some unknown signal.

Chile

- At the first introduction, a handshake is the customary greeting. Among close friends, an *abrazo* may also occur, along with a possible pat on the back. Men and women who are good friends, and two women, will kiss one cheek, usually the right one.

- Men should note that when a woman enters the room, the polite gesture is to rise and be prepared to shake her hand *if* she offers it. A seated woman, however, need not rise, nor is she obliged to offer her hand when a man enters.

- The customary Latin inclination toward closeness applies here, with people standing closer than North Americans or Europeans do.

- Maintain good eye contact.

- Good posture while seated is also important.

- Yawns should be stifled or covered with the hand.

- Waiters may be beckoned with hand gestures, but others are beckoned more discreetly.

- Some important gestures in Chile are:

  — Making a fist and slapping it up into the palm of the other hand is a very rude gesture.

  — Holding the palm upward and then spreading the fingers signals that someone is "stupid."

  — If a Chilean driver holds his hand out the window as if he is holding a round object, he is making an obscene gesture.

  — Holding the fist upright, level with the head, is a sign used by socialist and other leftist groups.

- When dining, one seldom eats anything with the fingers.

- If you pour wine, never do so with your left hand.

- Chilean wines are prized; if and when toasts are made, it is sufficient simply to raise your glass, look briefly at your host and others present, and say *"salud."*

Colombia

- A warm and friendly handshake is the custom in Colombia and is done frequently; especially on arriving and departing. Among male friends it will probably be a warm, friendly, and lingering handshake, often accompanied by lightly grasping the other's forearm or elbow. Among close male friends, the handshake may be preceded (or followed) with an *abrazo,* or hug, plus a couple of hearty claps on the shoulder or back.

- Colombian women will often substitute the gesture of holding forearms for a handshake.

- If you are visiting on business and happen to tour a factory, it is polite to shake hands with those workers nearest you.

- Etiquette and propriety are important in Colombia, therefore avoid placing your feet on a table or other piece of furniture, and avoid yawning in public and eating on the streets.

- To beckon someone, extend the arm, palm down, and move the fingers in a scratching motion.

- Some gestures that may be unique to Colombia are:

  — When using the hand to demonstrate how tall things are, the flat palm is held downward to show the height of *animals* but never people. To show the height of a person, the flat palm is held *sideways* (thumb on top).

  — To show the *length* of something, most visitors would put two hands out, pointing the two index fingers and letting the distance between the two fingers represent the distance. *This is considered a rude gesture in Colombia.* In Colombia, to show the length of something, hold the right arm out, palm flat 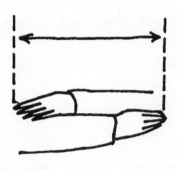 with thumb on top, and use the other hand to mark off the length along the right hand, wrist, or forearm.

  — Tapping the underside of the elbow with the fingers of the other hand suggests that someone is "stingy."

  — If a Colombian holds a hand out, palm flat and pointing downward, and then takes his other hand and makes a sawing motion across the back of the first hand, it is a way of saying "Let's share or split the profits."

  — Making the "O.K." signal with the thumb and forefinger making a circle, other fingers spread, and then placing the circle over your nose is a signal that someone else is a homosexual.

- When dining, many Colombians use the Continental style of eating, with the fork always remaining in the left hand.

- Toasting is a simple matter of raising the glass, looking around at those closest to you, and saying *"salud,"* which means "health."

- To indicate that you have finished eating, place the knife and fork horizontally across the plate.

- Women visitors should be especially sensitive about making any glance or gesture that might be considered flirtatious.

Costa Rica

- Men shake hands. Among good friends, men often hug and pat each other's shoulders after shaking hands. Costa Rican women pat left arms or shoulders. Women who are good friends will kiss cheeks. Rural people will offer a slight bow and touch their hats.

- In business situations, formality rules. Don't expect *abrazos* here, and suit jackets are usually kept on during business discussions.

- Exchange business cards, with yours printed in both English and Spanish.

- Don't ever put your feet up on any article of furniture.

- People usually queue in orderly lines for public transportation.

- Most American gestures—including rude ones—are known by Costa Ricans (who call themselves *"ticos"*). However, one gesture generally not used in the United States is the "fig" gesture: the hand is made into a fist and the thumb is forced upward to protrude between the forefinger and middle finger. This is a very rude gesture.

- When dining, conversation is common, but it is impolite to talk with food in the mouth or pick your teeth.

- Nude or partially nude sunbathing or swimming is regarded as extremely rude and improper.

Ecuador

- As in other Latin countries, the handshake is the custom upon both arrivals and departures. Good male friends will embrace (the *abrazo*) and good female friends will embrace and kiss lightly on the cheek.

- Also, as in many Latin countries, touching and closeness are common. When conversing with an Ecuadorian, don't be surprised if he or she stands what you regard to be as unusually close. Casual touching of arms and shoulders is usually just a sign of friendship.

- Fidgeting with the hands is considered distracting, almost impolite. Same with the feet.

- When beckoning a waiter, you may observe that some patrons will clap their hands over their heads, but that is generally considered rude.

El Salvador

- The handshake is the common form of greeting here. North Americans and Europeans, accustomed to rather brief handshakes, may notice that Salvadorans, like many Latins, linger over the handshake. There may also be casual touching of the forearm, shoulder, and elbow as an acquaintanceship grows. Males who are good friends will probably embrace, the *abrazo*. A common form of greeting among female friends in the middle and high social classes is to shake hands and brush cheeks as if kissing.

- Males are expected to rise from a seated position whenever a woman enters the room.

- Good eye contact is important in both social and business situations.

- Salvadorans are expressive with both hands and face, so watch for those signals that complement verbal communication.

- Yawning in social and business situations should be avoided.

- It is considered impolite to point the fingers at a person or group of people.

- Many other gestures commonly used and known throughout Latin America will be known in El Salvador, so be familiar with those and then be watchful to see if they are rigidly practiced or simply known but not in daily use.

Guatemala

- A "hearty handshake" is the description often given to greetings in Guatemala. But this does not necessarily mean a strong, firm grip. Latins tend toward a more gentle grip than practiced by North Americans and some Europeans. Close male friends will also greet with an *abrazo*, accompanied by patting the back. Close female friends will hug lightly and brush cheeks as if kissing.

- Greetings here should also be accompanied by good eye contact, a friendly smile, and genuine interest in the other person.

- It is best to ask permission before taking photographs of people. In fact, some people in the countryside will request a small payment in return.

- A soft voice is preferred to any loud, boisterous talking.

- To beckon someone, extend the arm, palm down, and move the fingers in a scratching motion.

- When waving good-bye, the proper gesture is to raise your hand *with the palm facing you,* and then wave your fingers together back and forth. When waving good-bye or thanks at a distance, raise and wave your hand *with the palm facing outward.*

- One gesture that should be avoided is the "fig" gesture. This is done by making a fist and then pushing the thumb up to protrude between the index and middle fingers. In some Mediterranean countries, this is considered a phallic symbol and is therefore terribly rude—as it is in Guatemala. However, in Brazil it is considered a sign meaning good luck.

- When being entertained, the female guest of honor will be seated to the right of the host and the male guest of honor at the host's left side.

- When dining, it is polite to finish everything on your plate.

- To attract a waiter, just raise your hand. In some less formal restaurants, patrons will make a sound like "cht, cht," but that is considered slightly impolite.

- Most North American gestures are understood in Guatemala.

Honduras

- As in most Latin countries, a warm but gentle handshake is the customary greeting. Close male friends will also embrace (the *abrazo*), while close female friends will hug lightly and offer a "pretend kiss" to the cheek.

- Personal space is smaller, and therefore North Americans and Northern Europeans may find Hondurans standing closer to them when conversing. This is merely a common trait and has no other significance.

- The "fig" gesture (hand making a fist with the thumb protruding between index and middle fingers) is an obscene and therefore insulting gesture.

- You may notice a Honduran waving an index finger back and forth in front of him, perhaps about chin level. This is a gesture signifying "no."

- If a Honduran takes one index finger, places it near the corner of his eye, and seems to tug downward gently, this is a signal that is saying "Be careful. Watch out." Some males also may do this at women to be flirtatious.

- Bargaining is expected when shopping.

- Most Hondurans will be aware of common North American gestures.

Mexico

- A warm, somewhat soft handshake is the customary greeting among both men and women. Men should let the woman make the first move toward handshaking. After the second or third meeting, Mexican men may begin with or add the *abrazo*, the embrace, along with a few pats on the back. Women friends will embrace lightly and kiss a cheek.

- In some areas of Mexico, you may encounter an unusual addition to the handshake where, after gripping the palm, the two people slide their hands upward to grasp each other's thumbs.

- Many Mexicans are touch-oriented. This means they may linger over a handshake, they may touch the forearm or elbow, or they may even casually finger the lapel of the other person's suit. All these touches merely signify a willingness to be friendly, nothing more.

- When gesturing to indicate the height of an animal, Mexicans will extend the arm out, *palm downward,* at the designated height. This should *not* be used for the height of people, however. Instead, Mexicans will use a raised index finger.

- To beckon others, extend the arm, palm down, with the fingers making a scratching motion inward.

- In restaurants, there are three common methods for getting the attention of a waiter. The first is to make a "pssst-pssst" sound; the second is to make a kissing sound with pursed lips. However, both of these, though common, are considered slightly impolite. A third, and more polite gesture, is to lift your arm and signal with your hand.

- While eating, both hands should be kept above the table, not in the lap.

- Mexicans are usually considered more open, more expressive than North Americans, particularly in northern Mexico.

- When passing an object to another person, hand it to him or her—don't toss it. The same is true when handing over change—don't put it on the counter, place it in the hand.

- In public, men should not stand with their hands in their pockets.

- If a man stands with his hands on his hips, it suggests hostility or a challenge.

- Deference is shown to the elderly, so give way to them in public places and don't object if they are waited on first.

- Ask permission before photographing local people.

- Bargaining in small- to medium-size stores, in outdoor markets, and with street vendors is natural and expected. But do not try to bargain in large stores.

- Never visit churches or religious sites while wearing short shorts, tank tops, or cutoff shirts or shorts.

- The national drink in Mexico is *tequila.* To drink it properly, here is the procedure: place a pinch of salt in the depression of your left hand between thumb and forefinger; then lick the salt and quickly take a drink of *tequila;* follow this by sucking on a lime wedge.

- A distinctive and very rude gesture in Mexico is as follows: make a **V** with the index and middle fingers with your palm facing you; then place the **V** over your nose.

- Patience is important; avoid showing anger if and when you encounter delays or interruptions.

- Nude bathing is very offensive to Mexicans. However, in rural areas it is not uncommon to see people bathing in rivers and creeks. Many homes lack indoor bathing facilities.

- Many gestures common in North America have been imported across the border into Mexico, so they will be understood and, in many cases, even used.

Nicaragua

- The typical warm, friendly Latin handshake prevails here. Men who are close friends will embrace (the *abrazo*), and women friends will engage in a brief hug and cheek-kissing motion.

- Smiles are important when meeting others, and North Americans and Europeans may find that Nicaraguans stand closer together during gatherings and conversations. This merely reflects the Latin attitude toward personal space.

- Deference and respect are shown to the elderly with many actions and gestures: rising when they enter the room, opening doors, and giving up seats on public transportation.

- As in other Central American countries, one obscene gesture is the "fig." This is the label given to the fist when the thumb protrudes upward between the index and middle fingers. It is a phallic symbol, and therefore considered an offensive and rude gesture.

- Eye contact is important at all times.

- Most American gestures are known here, with many of them in common daily use.

Panama

- A nod, a handshake, and the *abrazo* are all used in Panama for daily greetings. A nod and a mildly firm handshake are the most common, while the *abrazo*, or embrace, is frequently exchanged among good male friends. Women friends will embrace lightly, and make a kissinglike motion to one cheek.

- Women should avoid wearing clothing that is revealing.

- When dining, the host usually sits at one end of the table with the guest of honor at the other end.

- Because of the long U.S. presence in Panama, most American gestures will be known and understood.

Paraguay

- Handshaking is not only the common greeting but done, as in many Latin countries, on both arriving and departing. Men shake hands with other men and also with women. Women friends will embrace briefly and brush cheeks in a "pretend kiss."

- Paraguayans will usually stand very close to you during conversations.

- If you cross your legs while seated, cross them knee-over-knee instead of propping one ankle on top of the other knee.

- Try to keep your feet on the floor, and never prop them on a piece of furniture.

- Good, erect posture is important while seated, and don't sit on desks, tables, or other articles of furniture.

- If a Paraguayan brushes his fingers under his chin and then outward, he is saying "I don't know."

- When dining, the Continental style (fork constantly in the left hand) is customary here.

- Don't keep your hands in your lap while eating. Rest the wrists lightly on the table—but never the elbows.

- Exhibit patience in all your actions.

Peru

- Both men and women shake hands when greeting and when departing. Men who are good friends will add or even substitute an *abrazo*, or hug, accompanied by some hearty patting on the back. Women will hug lightly and brush cheeks as if kissing. Children will often kiss elders as a greeting, even if they have not met before. North Americans and Europeans may unintentionally perform what has been called the "conversational tango" with people in Peru. This is because Peruvians, and many other Latins, tend to stand very close together when conversing. This makes Americans and Europeans very uncomfortable, so they back off. The Latin follows, and the visitor retreats again. As a visitor, try to avoid this lest you silently signal to your "partner" that you don't like him or his conversation.

- Women in Peru may be seen walking arm-in-arm. This merely expresses friendship or a close relationship such as mother-daughter.

- When walking alongside a woman, "well-bred" men will walk with a protective hand under her elbow, which she should obligingly bend.

- In either social or business conversation, good eye contact is important.

- When seated, crossing the legs is acceptable, but it is customary to cross them at the knees—not with one ankle propped on the other knee.

- If you want to beckon someone, extend the arm, palm down, and wiggle the fingers in a scratching motion.

- If you smoke cigarettes, offer them to those around you before smoking. The same with candy.

- If and when photographing members of the Indian population, be certain to obtain permission first. The village mountain people believe photographing children will take away their souls.

- Tapping the index finger to the temple means he or she is crazy.

But tapping the index finger to the middle of the forehead means he or she is "dumb" or "stupid."

- Shaking the hand up and down at the wrist with the fingers flapping, if done slowly, means "What a lot!" But if done rapidly and with the elbow raised, it means "Oh, boy, we're in for it."

- Gestures noted in other Latin countries that are also used in Peru are:

  — Tapping the underside of the elbow with the fingers means "cheap" or "stingy."

  — Tugging the corner of the eye downward with a finger means "Be careful," or "Look out."

  — Pointing can be done by pursing the lips and motioning in the desired direction. Never point with the forefinger to a person or group of people. This is a sign of disrespect and poor breeding.

- When dining, keep your hands above the table. The best position is with wrists lightly on the table. No elbows on the table.

- To signal that you have finished eating, place your knife and fork in parallel across your plate.

Puerto Rico

- The handshake is the customary greeting here. Old friends may embrace, the *abrazo*. Women friends may embrace lightly and brush cheeks, as if kissing.

- As in most Latin countries, people tend to stand close to one another in any social or even business setting. This relates to a different perspective on personal space, with North Americans and many Europeans believing that people should stand about an arm's length from one another. If you tend to move away from a Latin, it could be considered as offensive or insulting.

- Some unique gestures to know in Puerto Rico are as follows:

  — Men tend to smile and stare at women, which is considered acceptable, but the reverse is not.

  — Puerto Ricans tend to interrupt each other frequently and are not upset when this occurs.

  — When handing small items to people, never toss or throw them.

— To beckon someone, the fingers are waved downward.

— If someone wiggles his or her nose, it probably means he or she is saying, "What's going on here?"

— To point, instead of using the hand and index finger, a Puerto Rican may purse the lips and motion toward the object with the mouth.

— You will hear restaurant patrons signal for waiters by making a "psssst" sound.

- Because of the close economic and political ties with the United States, most American gestures will be known and possibly used in parts of Puerto Rico.

Uruguay

- A warm and friendly handshake is the custom in Uruguay among both men and women. Good male friends will hug; women will do the same, adding a "pretend" kiss on the cheeks.

- When young people are introduced in Uruguay, girls may kiss one another, and boys may give brotherly kisses to the girls. Young men, however, will shake hands.

- Physical closeness is also common here, so people will stand close together in both social and business situations.

- To signal to a waiter, simply raise your hand. Some locals may make a kissing sound, but it is considered rude.

- Many North American gestures, as described in Chapter 2, will be recognized here. For example, the thumbs-up signal is well known and used in Uruguay. Similarly, because of its close proximity to Brazil, Uruguayans will consider the "O.K." symbol a very rude gesture.

Venezuela

- People greet one another here with a warm, somewhat gentle but friendly handshake. Men who know each other well may pat the right shoulder of the other person as well. Good male friends will embrace, the *abrazo*. Men and women who are good friends may kiss, and good women friends will hug lightly and kiss cheeks. Be sure to shake hands when arriving and when departing as well.

- Maintaining good eye contact during business or social discussions is considered both polite and important.

- As in many Latin countries, posture while seated is important. Try to keep the feet well planted on the floor, and avoid slouching or placing your foot on a chair or desk.

- When dining, wait for everyone else at the table to be served before beginning to eat.

- To indicate you have finished eating, place your utensils in parallel and diagonally across your plate.

- It is better to conduct business in person rather than over the telephone.

- Closeness and casual touching among males will be seen in Venezuela just as in most Latin countries. Men should be very careful about public physical contact with women, however.

UNITED STATES AND CANADA

Canada (Western and Atlantic Provinces)

- A firm handshake plus direct eye contact is the standard form of greeting in Canada. Men should shake hands with women if they offer their hand, but many women will just say "hello," perhaps with a nod of the head, and not shake hands.

- Distances are farther apart than in Latin America or the Far East. When conversing, people will stand about a half meter apart.

- There is little or no casual touching. The only exceptions are that good male friends may occasionally pat the other's back, close relatives may put their arms around another's shoulder, and good female friends may occasionally hug when greeting each other after long intervals.

- Good eye contact is important, whether it is during business or social conversation.

- In social situations, men will usually rise when women enter a room.

- Canadians in these provinces are described as "friendly," "somewhat reserved," and "on the conservative side." Therefore, excessive gesturing is not common.

- Men will sit with legs crossed, and all three forms are common and accepted: crossed at the ankles, crossed at the knees, and having one ankle crossed on the other knee.

- Beckoning is done by raising the hand, *fingers pointing up and palm inward*, and motioning the fingers toward one's face or body. This contrasts with the beckoning signal in many other parts of the world where the arm is extended, palm down, and the fingers are moved in a scratching motion.

- To beckon a waiter, just raise the hand at or above head level. To signal that you want the check, make a motion with the hands as if you are signing a piece of paper.

- Canadians may eat with either the Continental style (fork constantly in the left hand) or the American style (where the fork moves back and forth between the hands).

- Most of the popular gestures shown in Chapter 2 will be known, used, and fully understood in Canada. The one exception might be the "hook 'em horns" gesture known in the United States (especially in Texas), and in Italy, Africa, and Brazil.

Canada (Quebec)

- Since the French culture is so strong in this province, certain actions associated with Europe may be noted here. A firm handshake is still the common and preferred method of greeting, but it may be done more often (for example, at both arrivals and departures, and in all social situations). Also, close male friends may embrace lightly when meeting, and women may do the same, while adding a light kissing motion to the cheek.

- French-speaking Canadians may seem more reserved than their American neighbors to the south, with more emphasis on all aspects of etiquette.

- It is considered bad manners to eat while on the street.

- To beckon a waiter, nod the head backward slightly, or raise your hand discreetly.

- When dining, the Continental style of eating will probably prevail, although some Canadians will shift the fork back and forth American-style.

- Most of the more common gestures pictured in Chapter 2 will be known, understood, and even used by Québecois.

United States

- A firm handshake, accompanied by direct eye contact, is the standard greeting in the United States. Occasionally, among very good friends who have not seen one another for long intervals, women may briefly hug other women; and men may quickly kiss the cheek of a woman. Males rarely hug one another, however. Occasionally, men may shake hands with the left hand either covering the handshake or lightly gripping the forearm. This represents a higher degree of warmth and friendship, and politicians may be seen using this technique when campaigning.

- According to anthropologists, Americans tend to stand just about one arm's length away from each other while conversing or standing in public. It's called "the comfort zone."

- In the past decade, much emphasis has been placed on sexual equality in the workplace. While many women still enjoy having men open doors for them, help them get seated, and give up seats in public transportation, there are some women who object to such deference.

- Speaking of exceptions, because the United States has such ethnic diversity, visitors may also occasionally observe people greeting one another with hugs and cheek-kissing. Certain nationalities have brought these customs to the United States and continue to practice them, but they are not in wide use.

- Probably the only circumstance where two men may be seen walking in public and holding hands is if they are openly homosexual.

- Direct eye contact in both social and business situations is very important. Not doing so implies boredom or disinterest.

- Americans generally respect queues, or lines, in public situations and will form lines in an orderly fashion. To shove or push one's way into such a line will probably generate both anger and verbal complaints.

- There are two well-known rude and insulting gestures in the United States. Both are recognized in all parts of the country. They are:

— The middle finger thrust.

— The forearm jerk.

- Waving "hello" or "good-bye" is done by extending the arm, palm facing down, and waving the hand up and down at the wrist joint. Another variation is to raise the arm, palm outward, and move the whole arm and hand back and forth like an upside-down pendulum. This may be important to know because in many other countries this is a signal for "no."

- Many Americans become uncomfortable with periods of silence. Therefore in business or social situations, if a gap occurs, they will quickly try to fill in with conversation.

- Winking in the United States can signal diverse messages: flirtation, friendliness, amusement, or to signal "I am just kidding."

- When driving, automobiles are equipped with flashing lights as turning signals. If these are not operating, or if cyclists wish to signal for a turn, the proper procedure is as follows: extending the left arm straight out of the driver's window means "I plan to turn to the left," but if the arm is bent *upward* it signals "I plan to turn to the right."

- Beckoning can be done either by raising the index finger and repeatedly curling it in and out, or by raising the hand (palm facing inward) and waggling the fingers back toward the body. Either is acceptable.

- To call a waiter, just raise one hand to head level or above. To signal that you want the check, make a writing motion with two hands (one hand representing the paper, the other making a writing motion).

- When dining, many Americans are taught to keep the left hand in their lap and eat with the right hand. It is permissible to sit at a table with both wrists resting lightly on the table. When engaged in deep, close conversation, two people might even lean forward, with elbows on the table, but strict practitioners of etiquette in the United States frown on this.

- It is considered impolite to use toothpicks in front of other people.

- It has become an important courtesy in the United States to ask permission of your host or hostess before smoking.

- Using the hand and index finger to point at objects or to point directions is perfectly common and acceptable. However, pointing is sometimes considered rude if done very obviously.

- Two popular sports in the United States are baseball and football. Both have a special set of unique signals used by the officials—called umpires and referees, respectively—to indicate to onlookers what is happening on the playing field. A spectator can usually find the explanation for each of these signals in the printed program sold at such sporting events.

- To signal across a distance that "You have a telephone call," Americans will usually point at the person and then hold the other hand up to the jaw and mouth as if holding a telephone receiver.

- Whistling is common, either as a method for hailing the attention of someone at a distance, as an accompaniment to applause or cheering, or as a form of personal entertainment. However, it is not customarily done at formal events. Whistling is *not* intended as a form of vocal derision as it is, say, in Europe. In the United States, crowds voice disapproval by shouting out the word *booooo!*

- If an American is seen holding both hands to the throat, this is the signal for "I am choking." It might be seen, for instance, at sporting events as a sarcastic signal that someone is showing tension and playing poorly. But it can be used in a far more serious situation. Health experts in the United States are urging people to use—and to recognize—this gesture if and when a person is choking on a piece of food. In such a situation, the person cannot talk and is signaling "Help!"

- Mothers will scold children by shaking an index finger at them. People will admire children by patting them on the top of the head.

- One commonly used hand gesture for signaling "no" is to wave the forearm and hand (palm outward) in front and across the upper body, back and forth.

- Other popular gestures illustrated in Chapter 2, such as the "O.K." sign, "V" for Victory, and "thumbs-up," are all very popular and well known throughout the United States. The "hook 'em horns" gesture is associated with the state of Texas. The "hang loose" gesture is known and used in the state of Hawaii but not generally known in the other forty-nine states of the United States.

Additional Reading

Asian Customs and Manners, Kevin Chambers (Meadowbrook, 1988), is an excellent guidebook.

Bodytalk: The Meaning of Human Gestures, Desmond Morris (Crown Trade Paperbacks, 1994), features the illustrations, descriptions, and explanations of more than 600 common gestures from all parts of the world. Morris is, of course, the leading author in the field of human and animal behavior, with over thirty books to his credit.

Culture Shock (Times Books International, Singapore and Kuala Lumpur), an excellent series of books on several Far Eastern countries, including Thailand, Singapore, Malaysia, Korea, and Japan. Each is written by different authors and each is jammed with information on all aspects of culture and behavior for that country.

The Economist (Magazine) Business Traveller's Guides, (Prentice-Hall Press), are excellent handbooks when traveling or doing business internationally. Separate books have been published for the following areas: Britain, France, Germany, China, Japan, Southeast Asia, the United States, and the Arabian Peninsula.

European Customs and Manners, Nancy D. Braganti and Elizabeth Devine (Meadowbrook, 1984), is a fine guidebook.

Fundamentals of Nonverbal Behavior, edited by Robert S. Feldman and Bernard Rime (Cambridge University Press, New York, 1991), is the most recent compendium of serious research for academics in this field. The editors refer to "symbolic gestures, gestural systems, and sign language" when describing what has been termed in this text as "socially acquired gestures."

HarperCollins Business Guide to Moscow (HarperCollins, 1990). An indispensable guide to anyone traveling to that capital city.

Latin American Customs and Manners, Elizabeth Devine and Nancy L. Braganti (St. Martin's Press, 1988), is another excellent area-specific guidebook.

Looking at Each Other, Marion E. Current and Choi Dong-ho (Seoul International Tourist Publishing Co.), is a valuable handbook for anyone visiting South Korea or dealing with Koreans.

Multicultural Manners: New Rules of Etiquette for a Changing Society, Norine Dresser (Wiley, 1996), deals with all types of behavior among differing cultures. Dresser is a columnist for the *Los Angeles Times,* a folklorist, and an educator. Her book would be essential to anyone with more than a casual interest in cultural behavior.

Understanding Arabs, A Guide for Westerners, Margaret K. Nydell (Intercultural Press Inc., 1987), provides just what the title proposes.

The Web of Culture is a site on the Worldwide Web of the Internet developed by E. F. Sheridan. The e-mail address is:

http://www.worldculture.com

This site has grown rapidly in popularity and is cited by numerous Internet observers as a useful and informative resource. It offers entertaining contests and quizzes, chat groups, and resources for everything from books on cross-cultural matters to geographical data and consultants for hire.

Index